Into Textbooks
Into Writing

跟着教材学写作

李茂启　智敬谊　孙尧◎著

重庆大学出版社

图书在版编目(CIP)数据

跟着教材学写作 / 李茂启, 智敬谊, 孙尧著. --
重庆 : 重庆大学出版社, 2024.12
ISBN 978-7-5689-4483-0
Ⅰ. ①跟… Ⅱ. ①李… ②智… ③孙… Ⅲ. ①英语课
—高中—升学参考资料 Ⅳ. ①G634.413

中国国家版本馆 CIP 数据核字(2024)第 096786 号

跟着教材学写作

GENZHE JIAOCAI XUE XIEZUO

李茂启 智敬谊 孙 尧 著

责任编辑:罗 亚 版式设计:罗 亚

责任校对:关德强 责任印制:赵 晟

*

重庆大学出版社出版发行

出版人:陈晓阳

社址:重庆市沙坪坝区大学城西路 21 号

邮编:401331

电话:(023) 88617190 88617185(中小学)

传真:(023) 88617186 88617166

网址:http://www.cqup.com.cn

邮箱:fxk@ cqup.com.cn (营销中心)

全国新华书店经销

重庆新生代彩印技术有限公司印刷

*

开本:787mm×1092mm 1/16 印张:9.25 字数:272 千

2024 年 12 月第 1 版 2024 年 12 月第 1 次印刷

ISBN 978-7-5689-4483-0 定价:35.00 元

CONTENTS 目 录

第一章

写作背景与意义

一、《普通高中英语课程标准》对学生英语写作的要求

《普通高中英语课程标准(2017 年版 2020 年修订)》(以下简称“新课标”)指出,语言技能包含听、说、读、看、写等,其中听、看、读属于理解性技能,说和写属于表达性技能。这就要求学生运用语言技能理解语篇,并对语篇做出回应。

新课标对“写”的语言技能提出了以下要求。

在必修课程阶段,学生应能:

1. 使用文字手段描述个人经历和事物特征;
2. 在书面表达中借助标题、图标、图像、表格、版式等传递信息、表达意义;
3. 根据表达目的选择恰当的语篇类型、词汇和语法结构、正式或非正式语等。

在选择性必修课程阶段,学生应能:

1. 以书面形式描述、概括经历和事实;
2. 以书面形式传递信息、论证观点、表达情感;
3. 运用语篇衔接手段,提高表达的连贯性;
4. 根据表达的需要,设计合理的语篇结构;
5. 在书面表达中有目的地利用标题、图标、图表、版式、字体和字号等手段有效地传递信息、表达意义等。

在选修课程即提高类课程阶段,学生应能:

1. 通过书面方式再现想象的经历和事物;
2. 通过罗列、举例、对比等方式进行论证;
3. 根据需要使用委婉语、模糊语,使用衔接手段有效提高语篇的连贯性等。

从以上要求中我们可以看出,经过高中阶段的学习,在“写”的技能方面,学生应掌握和运用语篇衔接手段使写作连贯;在语篇类型方面,学生应掌握记叙文、说明文、议论文和应用文等不同类型的文体。对于记叙文,学生应能描述经历和事实。对于议论文,学生应能采用对比论证、举例论证、列举事实论证等多种论证方式来呈现和论证观点。对于应用文,学生应能根据表达需要选择合适的语体。

二、“三新”背景下,新教材呈现的写作文本和要求

普通高中各个学科的新课标优化了课程结构,增强了课程选择性,促进了教考的有效衔接。到 2022 年秋季学期,全国各省(区、市)已全面实施新课程、使用新教材,进入高考综合改革的 29 个省份均实现了新课程、新教材、新高考“三新”同步。

河南省于 2021 年秋季开始使用新教材。我校英语学科于 2021 年秋季开始使用人教版

新教材。其中,必修第一册至必修第三册教材中 Reading for Writing 板块的主要设计意图为:通过以读促写、读写结合的形式帮助学生学习语篇结构和语言特征;践行过程性写作模式,通过“学习—迁移运用”的过程,使学生将学习的语篇知识和语言知识迁移运用到新语境中;实现“教—学—评”一体化,强调同伴互评和自我评价,并提供相应的评价标准,提升学生的修改意识,培养其写作微技能。

教材配套练习册(Workbook)中,Writing 板块采用读写结合模式,为学生写作提供支架和写作指导(guided writing)。对阅读文本的深度阅读为学生写作提供语言支撑、语篇结构支撑和认知角度的支撑。此外,该板块为任务型写作模式,规定具体的写作任务目标和写作要求。最后,全套教材在写作体裁方面进行了系统的设计和安排,写作体裁丰富多样。

Book	Unit	Reading for Writing	Writing
必修第一册	Welcome Unit	A student profile	—
	Unit 1: Teenage Life	A letter of advice	A letter of advice
	Unit 2: Travelling Around	An email about Richard's travel plan	How to be a good tourist
	Unit 3: Sports and Fitness	A page in a wellness book	To propose a new sport or event to the IOC
	Unit 4: Natural Disasters	A summary of a news report	Write a summary of the text: *The Story of an Eyewitness*
	Unit 5: Languages around the World	A blog about English study	A short description of English learning experience
必修第二册	Unit 1: Cultural Heritage	A news report about cultural heritage protection	A news report about the Nanhai No. 1
	Unit 2: Wildlife Protection	A poster about an endangered species	A letter for help from WWF
	Unit 3: The Internet	A blog post about online safety	A comment about the blog post
	Unit 4: History and Traditions	A description of a beautiful or unusual place	Describe a historic city and the reason for recommending it
	Unit 5: Music	A speech about how music can change a person's life	Write your comments on a song or a piece of music

Continued

Book	Unit	Reading for Writing	Writing
必修第三册	Unit 1: Festivals and Celebrations	A narrative essay about a festival or celebration experience	An article about a festival or celebration
	Unit 2: Morals and Virtues	A review of a moral fable	Your own story about an act of kindness
	Unit 3: Diverse Cultures	An introduction to your city or town	A web page about symbols of China
	Unit 4: Space Exploration	An argumentative essay about space exploration	An essay about your opinions of humans living on Mars
	Unit 5: The Value of Money	A play script of a scene from *The Million Pound Bank Note*	A review of the play *The Million Pound Bank Note*

从必修教材的写作任务来看,主要包含以下体裁:

1. 记叙文:描写节日和庆祝习俗、关于“善良”主题的个人经历、描述英语学习经历;

2. 说明文:介绍所在的城市或城镇、描述一个美丽或与众不同的地方、描写一个历史文化名城;

3. 议论文:关于太空探索和人类在火星居住的观点、如何成为一个文明的游客、提出新体育项目或体育赛事;

4. 书信:建议信、旅行计划、求助信;

5. 概要写作:新闻报道和小说 *The Story of an Eyewitness* 的概要写作;

6. 演讲稿:音乐改变个人生活;

7. 新闻报道:关于文化遗产保护和“南海一号”的新闻报道;

8. 评论:评论 *The Million Pound Bank Note*、对道德有关故事的评论、对最喜欢的歌曲和音乐的评论、对博客的评论;

9. 网页文章:学生简介、健康书中的一页、关于中国元素的网页;

10. 博客:关于英语学习的博客、关于网络安全的博客;

11. 海报:设计关于动物保护的海报;

12. 剧本:基于 *The Million Pound Bank Note* 创作新剧本。

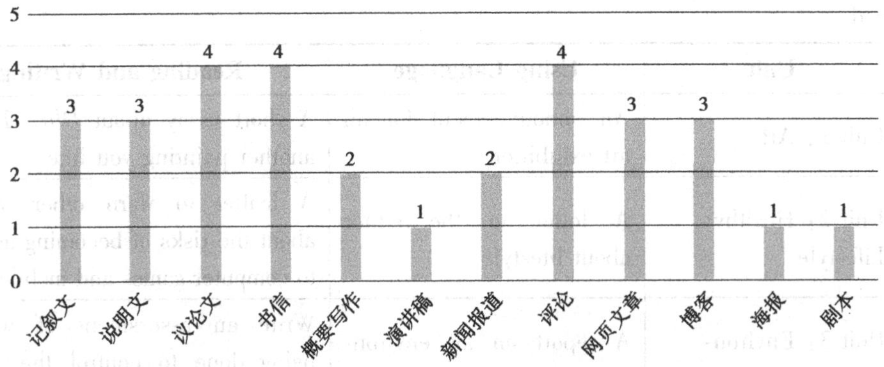

必修教材的写作板块共包含31篇写作训练。从上面的图表可以看出，必修教材的写作以议论文、书信、评论、记叙文、说明文、网页文章和博客为主，而概要写作、新闻报道等训练较少。

选择性必修教材的写作任务呈现在 Using Language 和 练习册（Workbook）中的 Reading and Writing 板块。

Book	Unit	Using Language	Reading and Writing
选择性必修第一册	Unit 1：People of Achievement	A description of someone you admire	Describe a hero in your eyes with examples and his/her influence
	Unit 2：Looking into the Future	An opinion essay about changes caused by technology	A report about whether to clone a particular animal or not
	Unit 3：Fascinating Parks	An introduction to a park	An email about your trip to Shangri-La with details
	Unit 4：Body Language	A description of body language	A story about a cat and a girl based on the pictures
	Unit 5：Working the Land	An argumentative essay on farming	An essay about advantages and disadvantages of working in the city or country
选择性必修第二册	Unit 1：Science and Scientists	An opinion essay about the scientific spirit	How science and technology have influenced your daily life
	Unit 2：Bridging Cultures	An argumentative letter about studying abroad	Reply to an ad by inviting Jim to stay at your home
	Unit 3：Food and Culture	A descriptive essay about one's diet	An essay on whether you prefer fresh food or prepared food
	Unit 4：Journey across a Vast Land	An email about a journey	A short essay about a long journey
	Unit 5：First Aid	A narrative essay about providing first aid	An advice leaflet to make your school safer

Continued

Book	Unit	Using Language	Reading and Writing
选择性必修第三册	Unit 1: Art	An announcement for an art exhibition	A short essay about *Olive Trees* or another painting you like
	Unit 2: Healthy Lifestyle	A letter to the editor about lifestyle	A leaflet to warn other students about the risks of becoming addicted to computer games and mobile games
	Unit 3: Environmental Protection	A report on an environmental issue	Write an assessment of what is being done to control the "small waste" problem
	Unit 4: Adversity and Courage	An essay about the story of Shackleton and his men on the ship *Endurance*	A story about someone who persevered and overcame adversity
	Unit 5: Poems	A poem	An essay about your understanding of the poem
选择性必修第四册	Unit 1: Science Fiction	A sci-fi short story	A summary of *Journey to the Center of the Earth*
	Unit 2: Iconic Attractions	A description of an iconic animal	Food from your hometown with a recipe
	Unit 3: Sea Exploration	An argumentative essay on sea exploration	An argumentative essay on sea protection
	Unit 4: Sharing	A speech about China's aid to other countries	A short description of your gift catalogue
	Unit 5: Launching Your Career	An application letter and a CV	An essay to express your opinion on how to be an expert

选择性必修教材写作任务的体裁包含：

1. 说明文：描述钦佩的人物、描述心中的英雄及原因、介绍国家公园、描述肢体语言、描述图画、描述个人饮食、描述画作、描述一种标志性动物、介绍家乡的美食、描述赠礼目录；

2. 记叙文：描写关于香格里拉的旅行、描述一次长途旅行、描述急救经历、描述某人坚持并克服逆境的故事、科幻故事；

3. 议论文：谈论科技带来的改变、谈论关于农业的观点、谈论在农村或者城市工作的优缺点、关于科学精神的观点、关于科技如何影响生活、关于申请出国学习的优缺点、谈论喜欢新鲜食物还是预制食物、对诗歌的理解、关于海洋开发的观点、关于海洋保护的观点、谈论如何成为专家；

4. 书信：如何使校园更安全的建议信、申请信和简历、答复信、关于旅行的邮件、写信介绍生活方式；

5. 演讲稿：中国对其他国家援助的演讲；

6. 报道：关于是否应克隆动物的报道、关于环境问题的报道；

7. 诗歌：一首诗歌；

8. 通知：艺术展览通知；

9. 传单：沉迷于电脑游戏和手机游戏的危害；

10. 评论：关于 small waste 问题解决措施的评论、对 Shackleton 的评论；

11. 概要：《地心之旅》的故事梗概。

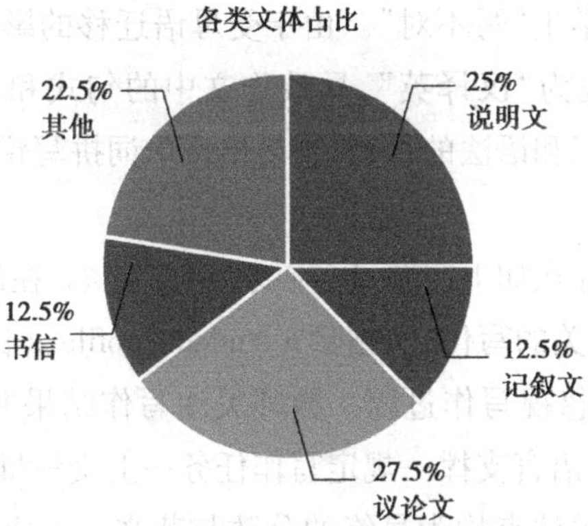

选择性必修教材共计 40 篇写作训练，体裁丰富。议论文和说明文占比较高，分别达 27.5%和 25%。与必修教材相比，议论文和说明文的比重明显上升，这也对学生的思维品质和思维能力提出了更高的写作要求。

三、高考对英语写作的考查

随着“三新”改革，英语试卷的结构也进行了调整，加大了写作的考查比重。自 2016 年开始考查的“读后续写”题型对学生的英语写作能力提出了更大的挑战，要求学生在规定时间内完成由原来的 100 词改为 230 词的写作。基于协同写作，“读后续写”体裁均为记叙文。该类型题目要求学生在阅读一篇 300 词左右的文章的基础上续写文本，并要求学生的写作兼具创意性与协同性。

写作考查	旧高考	新高考	
题目类型	应用文	应用文	读后续写
分值	25 分	15 分	25 分
词数	100 词左右	80 词左右	150 词左右

四、高中英语写作“学”与“教”面临的困境

英语写作既是学生学习的难点，也是教师教学的难点和重点。

学生被“不愿写”“不会写”“写不对”等问题困扰。首先，学生“不愿写”。学生对写作缺乏兴趣。写作耗费时间和精力，教师批改不及时等，都会导致学生在日常学习中谈起作文便面露难色。阅卷时，教师不难发现学生写作空白和抄袭阅读理解等文章的情况。其次，学生“不会写”。对于应用文写作，教师阅卷时不难发现，学生生搬硬套“模板”和“万能句型”。读后续写中，学生续写的故事情节扑朔迷离，存在随意添加人物、第一段和第二段甚至与原文没有关联等问题。最后，学生“写不对”。由于受母语迁移的影响，大部分学生采用“翻译式”写作的方法，即将写作视为“汉译英”，导致作文中的句式和词汇不符合英文的表达习惯。同时，由于学生缺乏词汇和语法的积累，容易出现单词拼写错误、语法错误等，导致作文词不达意，总体得分较低。

就教师而言，写作教学存在如下问题：1. 应试为主。比如，在课堂上只教授议论文、说明文和记叙文等与考试息息相关的写作，而删除 a student profile、a poster 等考试较少考查的体裁。2. 重视“结果性”写作，忽视写作过程。教师关注写作结果并强调写作结果的标准性。目前，大多数教师采用“提供语言支撑—规定写作任务—上交—批改—反馈共性问题—背范文”的模式。学生和教师的关注点均为最终的分数与范文。一次作文训练以范文背诵的完成为节点，因而忽视了学生写作能力的训练。3. 严重依赖教师批改，忽视学生的主体性。无论是日常习作还是考试作文，评判学生作品的主要甚至唯一途径为教师批改。虽然鼓励学生自评、互评作文，但是结果通常不尽如人意。大量的作文会导致出现批改不及时、只打分、只关注语言正确等问题。教师对学生的写作思维和写作技能关注较少。

基于以上背景，一线教师不仅需具备有效指导学生写作的能力，而且要将写作与日常教学融合，重视写作过程和语言积累。因此，本书以教材中的写作训练为基础，整合不同教材中出现的相似的写作体裁和话题，总结词汇和语言表达，为学生提供写作支架，为一线教师提供写作教学指导。

第二章

理论基础

第一节　理论综述

一、课程标准及高考评价体系

根据《普通高中英语课程标准》(2017 年版 2020 年修订),英语教学的重要使命是培养学生的核心素养,表现在语言能力、文化意识、学习能力和思维品质四个维度。深入研究教材中的多模态语篇,挖掘同体裁文本的共同特征,引导学生进行逻辑性、批判性的思考和阅读活动,能使学生获得英语学科的必备知识和关键学习能力。国外原版教材和国内多版本教材的碰撞能促进文化的交流、共享、互补、传承和传播,并能塑造学生科学全面的价值观、世界观和人生观,促进核心素养的形成。具体来说,多种教材的文章能促使学生挖掘文本特征、分析文章中的表意手段,沉浸式的阅读也能更好地培养学生的英语语感。另外,通过演绎、归纳、对比、解释等方法,学生能获取不同文本的精华,形成自己的观点,从而使思维能力得到提升。

此外,根据高考评价体系,教师在教学及命题中可重点关注学生获取知识的能力群、发展思维的能力群、实践操作的能力群的培养和评价。在众多英语教材的文本中,引导学生进行文本特点的研读有利于开发学生的逻辑思维和辩证思维能力。通过类似的情境化写作任务,学生可以将所吸收的知识内化并进行迁移。通过教材学习写作的思路对于英语人才的培养和高考的应试准备也是十分有意义的。

二、建构主义理论

长久以来,建构主义理论(Constructivism)在教育中起着举足轻重的作用,影响着各个层次、各个科目的教育教学。苏格拉底的"产婆术"是建构主义教学的典型例子。建构主义理论所推崇的教学过程一般包括情境、合作、对话及意义建构。维果茨基提出的"最近发展区"理论对建构主义理论的发展具有重要影响。简单来说,学生主动地学习并进行知识的重组、加工及建构,是建构主义理论的主要内涵。学生在学习过程中进行高水平的思维活动,综合和转换头脑中已有的知识与经验,从而对新问题、新现象、新话题做出科学合理的解释。

从阅读到写作的迁移与建构主义理论对情境性认知的强调是相一致的。按照本书的理念,教师提供给学生的来源于多版本教材的文本正如解决问题的原型,教师引领学生进行文本分析的过程正是进行学习探索的过程。学生之间的互动、教师与学生之间的互动正是交互作用的体现,这也是建构主义理论所极力倡导的。学生从阅读多版本教材文本到完成写作任务的真实情境,正是知识建构和迁移的过程。

三、脚手架理论

脚手架理论(Scaffolding Theory)的基础是建构主义理论,它是建立在维果茨基的"最近发展区"理论基础上的。教师在教学中应该努力缩小学生已有的知识水平和新知识之间的距离,实现最近发展区的跨越。脚手架理论使我们联想到有形的脚手架。"脚手架"指的是教师在教学中通过良好的互动学习,引导学习者达到学习目标的教学策略(倪娜,2012)。在教学中,教师确实可以借助一些支撑,使复杂的教学活动变得有章可循、易于攻破。写作教学亦是如此。本书的理论依据之一便是脚手架理论。从阅读出发,分析文章的结构,解析其写作技巧,是一个解构的过程,也好像是把一座摩天大楼拆解,发现其内部构造。写作是一个再构的过程,教师可通过创造可迁移的情境,引导学生从目前的写作水平进入更高的写作水平,实现最近发展区的跨越。

四、KWL 策略及 KWLSW 策略

唐娜·奥格尔(Donna Ogle)提出了阅读教学的 KWL 策略,重点突出学生已经掌握的知识(What I Know)、想知道的知识(What I Want to Know)和学会的知识(What I Have Learned)。杨峰(2023)在自己的教学研究中,将 KWL 策略发展为 KWLSW 策略,即在原来的基础上增加了 Share 和 Write 两个要素。在操作中,教师借助头脑风暴的形式调动学生的背景知识、激发学习热情。学生反馈头脑风暴中的认知矛盾、与话题相关的已知内容和想要了解的内容。学生在学习之后可以采用总结和知识地图的形式归纳从文本中学到的信息。学生在此基础上进行批判性的思考,对比想知道的内容和学到的内容。随后的分享环节中,学生以口头或书面的形式分享学习所得。最后,学生基于前面的学习阶段完成写作练习。

这两种教学策略通过规范的操作环节帮助学生实现从已知到未知,从阅读到口头或书面形式的分享,最后到写作的学习过程,体现了教与学的一致性,具有科学性和可操作性。从已知到未知,把未知变为已知,也是本书的核心思想。

五、POA 理论

产出导向理论(POA,product-oriented approach)是文秋芳(2017)提出的,它的基础是梅里尔·斯旺(Merrill Swain)的"输出假说",目的是提高课堂教学效率,解决英语课堂中的

“学用分离”等弊病,进而促进我国英语课堂教学效率的提升。产出导向理论能帮助学生学习英语知识,使学生能在真实环境中正确地使用英语。这一理论体系减小了输入与输出的距离,促进了陈述性知识与程序性知识之间的循环,是一套具有中国本土特色的教学理论。它包括三个教学理念:学习中心、全人教育及学用一体。教学假设包括输入驱动、输入促成和选择性学习。教学流程主要包括驱动、促成和评价。教师在教学过程中扮演着设计者、引领者和组织者的多种角色。广大高中学生在写作过程中面临着输出困难的现状,常常是词到用时方恨少,作文的句子结构偏单一。来源于多版本教材的相同体裁的文本正是打通学生输入和输出之间任督二脉的一剂良药。

第二节　KEDSTW 写作教学策略

传统的英语写作教学往往是被忽略的,或者处于一种无保障、无规划的状态,没有具体的、操作性强的教学策略。稍好一些的情况是,教师以填鸭的方式给学生灌输优秀的写作句式和范文,期望学生在死记硬背之后能在写作时想起来运用。但是,由于缺乏鲜活的语境,学生理解这些句式和范文并不容易,背诵效率低,不能做到内化和灵活运用。在以上两种写作教学中,写作的过程被忽略,学习的过程被简单化。在信息互通、知识浩如烟海的现代,写作教学策略如何才能与时俱进?

广大学者和一线教师的不同的教学理论,也给英语写作教学的探索提供了很多启示。基于上一节所阐述的理论,我们在教学探索中逐渐摸索出跟着教材学习写作的 KEDSTW 写作教学策略。下面简单介绍该教学策略的几个教学步骤:

产出导向理论所涵盖的“学习中心、学用一体”的理念对于写作教学具有指导意义。写作教学的产出是各类体裁的文章,这是本书中的教学设计的终点,亦是起点。教师可以将同类体裁文章的特点进行归纳和类别解析,并给学生简单介绍。此步骤可作为写作的第一步:类别解析。

“学习中心”的理念则指明,要完美达到产出的终点,我们可以选择各类体裁的鲜活语篇,而各个版本的教材无疑是科学、规范的语篇的不二之选。这也与建构主义理论、脚手架理论等是一致的。教材中各类体裁的文本是略高于习得者目前英语水平的语言材料,难易适中。在教学中,教师可对各类体裁的文本进行精细研读,发掘该体裁文章的文本特点,再基于文本分析进一步探索典型的课例。此步骤可作为广大教师在写作教学中的第二步和第三步:精研文本、课例展示。

在指导学生对同体裁的教材文本进行精细研读之后,教师可指导学生对文本中所蕴含的写作技巧进行探讨和归纳。结合教材的详细语境和不同版本教材中富有趣味性的文本，学生此时已经有了一定的"脚手架"作为支撑，这比干瘪的句式总结更具有情境依托。在这样的语料滋养下，学生能对各种体裁的写作有更系统、深刻的认识，更好地实现知识的总结和内化。此步骤可作为第四步：技巧归纳。

在学生与各版本教材中的同体裁文章进行了深入的碰撞之后，教师可创设类似的写作情境，鼓励学生进行写作迁移和创新。这也与新课标所倡导的英语学习活动观相一致。在前面的步骤中，学生一直都在进行学习理解和思考评判，为自己的写作奠定了基础，也为知识的建构提供了平台。结合教师创设的情境，学生可以逐渐摆脱"脚手架"，进阶到第五步：迁移创新。

学生的写作也是不断试错的过程，从最初的构思到写下草稿，经历着已有知识水平和目标语言水平（教材中的语言水平）的碰撞。需要指出的是，学生的写作是一个过程，在写作完成之后，需要结合多种方式进行评价。文秋芳（2018）提出了"师生合作评价"的形成性评价方式。事实上，生生互评、教师评价都可以在很大程度上促成作品的蝶变。特别是教师评价之后，学生还可以进一步完善作品，实现写作水平的质的提升。此步骤可作为第六步：作品舞台。

上述写作教学的思路大致可归纳为以下六个步骤：类别解析（Know）、精研文本（Extract）、课例展示（Demonstrate）、技巧归纳（Summarize）、迁移创新（Transfer）、作品舞台（Write）。为了指代方便，简称为 KEDSTW 写作策略，如下表所示。

K	E	D	S	T	W
类别解析	精研文本	课例展示	技巧归纳	迁移创新	作品舞台
Know	Extract	Demonstrate	Summarize	Transfer	Write

第三章

策略运用与建议

第一节　介绍人物

一、音容笑貌画形象，语言动作表感受

（一）类别解析

人物形象的塑造通常是通过外貌描写、表情描写、语言描写、动作描写、心理描写这几个方面来展现，而且经常需要综合使用多种描写。比如，心理描写往往也包含动作描写和表情描写，因为外在表情和动作是人物内心感受的反映。外貌描写如果只写人的五官长相，就像是在描述一幅挂在墙上的画，是静态的，缺少生命力和个性特点，但是如果加入一些表情神态的描写，就会立刻显得生动、传神，人物形象跃然纸上。刻画立体丰满、个性鲜明的人物形象需要灵活使用这几种描写手法。

（二）精研文本

新剑桥第三册第二单元 Speak and Read 板块中的 *Gelert—The Faithful Dog* 一文讲述的是一只忠心护卫主人的狗的故事。主人 Prince Llewellyn 外出打猎，把家里的婴儿交给狗狗 Gelert 看护。途中主人听见 Gelert 的叫声，赶紧调转马头返回家中，却发现婴儿不见了，而 Gelert 的嘴角和婴儿床上都有血迹。主人误以为是 Gelert 咬死了自己的儿子，一怒之下拔剑杀了 Gelert。这时婴儿床下传来一阵啼哭声，主人过去查看，发现婴儿安然无恙，地上还有一只满身血迹的狼的尸体。至此主人才明白，Gelert 没有杀死自己的孩子，而是击退狼的攻击，保护了自己的孩子。后悔不已的主人为 Gelert 修建坟墓并举行了隆重的葬礼，还每天到墓前看望。作者在讲述这个故事时运用了大量的动作描写，使故事犹如电影一般历历在目，画面感极强。紧凑的情节和悬念吸引着读者一直阅读到文章结尾，以令人意外的结局结束全文。我们来看一下文章中表现人物动作的词汇都有哪些：

While the Prince and his men were **riding through the forest**, they **heard** a loud barking… He **turned his horse around** and **galloped** quickly home… When Prince Llewellyn **walked through the door**, …The Prince **looked at** Gelert… When he **looked closer** he saw blood dripping from the dog's mouth and fur. Llewellyn **ran into** his son's bedroom… He **took his sword** and **swung it at the dog**… As Prince Llewellyn **look at** his dead dog on the floor he knew that he had done something wrong. He **looked around the room** and he saw that there had been a fight… And then he **heard the sound** of a baby crying… The Prince slowly **lifted it up**. He **organized** a great ceremony to **bury the dog**… He **visited** the grave every day until he died.

骑马穿过树林、听见狗叫声、飞驰返家、穿过房门、仔细查看、拔剑、挥剑、环视房间、举起、埋葬……作者运用这一系列动作描写，生动地勾勒出篇幅短小却情节紧凑的一篇故事来。

新概念第三册中课文的语言特点主要体现在它的真实性和情境性上，充满生活情趣。一个个生动有趣的小故事，充满了动作链的描写，极具画面感。第六课 *Smash and Grab* 一文讲述两个劫匪到珠宝店抢劫的故事。在这篇文章中有很多典型的动作描写，使得整个抢劫犯罪活动节奏紧张、扣人心弦：

The silence was suddenly **broken** when a large car, with its headlights on and its horn blaring, **roared down** the arcade. It **came to a stop** outside the jeweler's. One man **stayed** at the wheel while two others with black stockings over their faces **jumped out** and **smashed** the window … the men **scrambled** back into the car and it **moved off** at a fantastic speed. Just as it was leaving, Mr Taylor **rushed out** and **ran after** it **throwing** ashtrays and vases.

这段文字中，the silence was broken、came to a stop、stay at the wheel、jumped out、smashed the window、scrambled back into the car、moved off、rushed out、ran after 等一系列动作的描写，通过准确的用词、细致的刻画，让人感到画面感扑面而来。在描写动作时，很多学生只会使用一个动词粗略地概括整个动作，缺少细节，读起来难免枯燥无味，无法给人留下深刻的印象。在写作中我们要想象自己置身情境中，细化动作，即把动作过程分解成一连串(2~3 个)细微的动作并形成动作链，写出动作的连贯性。这样我们的描写就有了画面感，人物也更加立体。

新剑桥第四册第二单元 People Are People 的写作部分是一篇关于人物外貌和性格描写的典型文本。文本是写给好友的一封 Email，讲述了作者在周末聚会上偶遇一位非常有趣的男士(Harry)的经历。文中描写了 Harry 给作者留下的美好的第一印象，涉及了大量的人物外貌和性格描写。通过这篇文本我们可以看到，描写人物外貌不需要面面俱到，只需写出人物独特而有个性的部分，即可给人留下深刻印象，描写过多反而会模糊了人物形象，不够鲜明。而人物的性格往往也要通过列举人物的行为来表现，比如文中：

Harry must be the **best-looking** guy I've ever met. I mean he's **gorgeous**. He's **average height**. … was his **amazing blue eyes**. They're bright blue, like **the color of the ocean** you see in those holiday postcards… He's got **a great smile** too. It's **warm and friendly** and you can't help liking him immediately… He's a very **nice** guy too. He's a very **charming** person and he **made me feel good** about myself. He said **loads of nice things** about me… He came across as really **being interested in me**. I told him all about my problems with Lucy and **he really listened**. He was so **sympathetic** and he gave me some **good advice** too.

通过文中这些描写，一位长相帅气且笑容温暖的年轻小伙子就出现在我们眼前。他魅力十足又善解人意，耐心倾听又极富同情心，难免让人一见如故。

（三）课例展示

教材：新剑桥第三册第十一单元 Love 中的文本 *A Service of Love*

文本分析：本文是一篇短篇小说，改编自美国著名短篇小说家欧·亨利的著作，讲述了贫穷却热爱艺术的年轻夫妻 Delia 和 Joe，为了成全对方的艺术梦想而不得不放弃各自挚爱的艺术追求的感人故事，表现了 19 世纪美国草根阶层生活的无奈与艰辛，也体现了两个年轻人对艺术的追求和成就彼此的牺牲精神。文章中有大量人物描写，比如故事开篇对人物的介绍使用了外貌描写和性格描写：

Delia was a **young** pianist with **long**, **slender fingers** and **blonde hair**—and **a kind**, **generous nature**. Her husband Joe was a **promising** young painter—**broad-shouldered**, with **bushy eyebrows** and a wide smile—and **an honest**, **hardworking young man**.

当 Delia 无力支付高昂的钢琴课学费而决定放弃学习钢琴，同时迫于生活的窘迫决定去给一个女孩做家庭钢琴教师来维持生活时，作者使用了语言描写来表现丈夫 Joe 对此的态度和 Delia 做出的决定：

"Delia," **Joe said**, "I'd be much happier if you kept up your lessons." Delia said that it didn't matter. **She said**: "When I've earned some money, I'll start again. When you love your art, nothing's too much."

后来 Joe 为了让 Delia 宽心，谎称卖画挣了钱，有了不错的收入，使得两人的生活条件暂时有了改善，但很快又出现了新的问题。这里作者使用了心理描写和表情描写：

So the two of them were **happy** for a while. They didn't have to **worry** any more about finding the money to buy food and pay the bills. They missed their lessons, but that **didn't seem to matter**... She tried not to tell him, but then the **tears** began.

教学目标)))

1. 根据小说六要素，对故事内容、情节和细节进行梳理，增强学生对小说的阅读理解能力；

2. 通过人物描写的常见手法，找到体现人物情感的表达，提炼出故事的情感线，体会人物在不同人生境遇下的情感反应和变化；

3. 分析、解读小说标题的含义和语言特点。

教学重点)))

1. 如何通过阅读活动使学生对故事的人物和情节有比较准确的理解；
2. 如何发散学生的思维，引导学生结合自身生活经历思考问题的多种解决办法；
3. 如何使学生感受主人公对艺术的热爱，以及努力成全彼此的牺牲精神。

教学步骤)))

Activity 1：Warming up

Think of films, stories or poems about love. Can you talk about a love story in them?

What are the things that usually happen in a love story?

引入话题，引导学生思考电影、小说、诗歌中描绘的爱情故事中常发生的矛盾与冲突都有哪些，为下面的阅读做好铺垫。

Activity 2：Prediction

Look at the pictures and describe what you see.

Can you guess what the story is about?

让学生观察插图，发现其中的特别之处，并以此为线索猜测文本的内容。同时，结合学生的回答，板书讲解文本中的生词 blonde, slender, broad-shouldered, pianist, bushy, wrapped in bandage。

Activity 3：Reading

1. Read the text quickly to check your ideas. What is the story mainly about?
2. Read the text again and find out the basic elements of the story.

   Who was Delia? Who was Joe?

   Where were they?

   What was the problem they were facing? (Why did Delia and Joe stop taking lessons?)

   How did they solve their problem? (What did they say about how they were making money? What did they actually do to make money? How did Joe find out Delia was lying about her hand?)

   Why did they lie to each other?

   阅读文本，概括故事大意。根据小说六要素，引导学生梳理、理解故事情节。

Activity 4：Analysis and evaluation

1. How did they feel about their life? How did it change?
2. Do you think Joe and Delia were wrong to tell each other lies? Why or why not? What

would you do if you were Joe or Delia?

3. Do you think this is a happy story or a sad one? Why?

引导学生从文章中找到表现人物情感的表达，从而描绘出故事的情感线，分析人物情感的变化。启发学生思考故事中的人物在处理问题时使用的方式是否合理、正确，讨论还有哪些更好的方式，培养学生的分析能力和批判性思维能力。最后，让学生根据故事的开头和结尾来评价文章是喜剧还是悲剧，并说出原因。这里可以补充背景知识：欧·亨利式的结尾。

Activity 5: Discussion

1. How would you complete the two sentences at the end of the story?
2. What does "service" mean in the title *A Service of Love*?

通过让学生补全文章最后一句话来加深学生对故事主题的理解。结合故事内容、人物形象、主题意义等，鼓励学生谈论自己对标题中 service 一词的理解。

（四）技巧归纳

人物的外貌描写通常包括身高体型、五官长相、衣着打扮、发型首饰等，其中五官长相又分为眉、眼、口、鼻、耳、牙齿、肤色、脸型、睫毛、头发等。外貌描写一般不必面面俱到，只需要抓住人物最突出的特征进行刻画，突出人物的特点即可。如果不厌其烦地描写一个人外貌的所有细节，反而会让读者感到抓不住重点，很难在脑海中想象出人物到底是什么样子的，也不利于人物鲜明形象的塑造。比如 *Gone with the Wind* 中关于斯嘉丽的描写，寥寥几笔就描绘出一位皮肤白皙、睫毛浓密、有着淡绿色眼睛的少女的形象。

Scarlett O'hara was not beautiful... But it was **an arresting face**, **pointed of chin**, **square of jaw**. **Her eyes were pale green** without a touch of hazel, starred with **bristly black lashes** and slightly tilted at the ends. Above them, her **thick black brows** slanted upward, cutting a startling oblique line in her **magnolia-white skin**... Her **new green flowered-muslin dress** spread its twelve yards of billowing material over her hoops and exactly matched the **flat-heeled green morocco slippers** her father had recently brought her from Atlanta. The dress set off to perfection the **seventeen-inch waist**, the smallest in three counties, and the **tightly fitting basque** showed breasts well matured for her sixteen years. But for all the modesty of her spreading skirts, the **demureness of hair netted smoothly into a chignon** and the quietness of small white **hands folded in her lap**, her true self was poorly concealed. The **green eyes** in the carefully **sweet face** were **turbulent**, **willful**, **lusty with life**, distinctly at variance with her decorous demeanour.

再比如小说 *Oliver Twist* 中，描写了一位有着深蓝色眼睛和纯洁欢快笑容的 17 岁少女，她身形纤细、纯洁美丽，就像是一位不食人间烟火的仙子，让人联想到世间的一切美好。

She was not past seventeen. Cast in so **slight and exquisite** a mould, **so mild and gentle**, **so pure and beautiful**, that earth seemed not her element, nor its rough creatures her fit companions. **The very intelligence that shone in her deep blue eye and was stamped upon** her *noble head*, *seemed scarcely of her age or of the world*, *and yet the changing* **expression of sweetness and good humour**, the thousand lights that played about the face and left no shadow there; above all, the smile—**the cheerful happy smile**—were entwined with the best sympathies and affections of our nature.

"微笑"的常见英语表达:

快活的微笑 a bright smile
开朗的微笑 a broad smile
迷人的微笑 a charming smile
奸笑 a cunning smile
幸福的微笑 a happy smile
令人神往的微笑 an engaging smile
一丝微笑 a faint smile
愉快的微笑 a pleasant smile
满意的微笑 a pleased smile
不自然的微笑 a strained smile
甜蜜的微笑 a sweet smile
苦笑 a wry smile
狞笑 a grim smile
天真的微笑 an innocent smile
和蔼的微笑 a kind smile
轻蔑的微笑 a contemptuous smile

"嗓音"的常见英语表达:

清晰的嗓音 a clear/ringing voice
低沉的嗓音 a deep voice
响亮的嗓音 a loud voice
低音 a low voice
悦耳动听的嗓音 a pleasant voice
尖利刺耳的嗓音 a shrill voice
温柔的嗓音 a soft voice
甜美的嗓音 a sweet voice
尖细的嗓音 a thin voice
喑哑的嗓音 a toneless voice
微弱的嗓音 a weak/feeble voice
高音 a high voice
假嗓音 a falsetto voice
美妙的嗓音 a fine voice

"步态"的常见英语表达:

轻盈的步伐 a light gait
沉重的步伐 a heavy gait
昂首阔步的步伐 a swaggering gait
驼背弯腰的步态 a stooping gait
摇摇摆摆的步态 a swaying gait
一瘸一拐的步态 a limping gait
缓慢的步态 a shuffling gait
微跛的步态 a halting gait
文雅的步态 a mincing gait

"身材"的常见英语表达:

优美的身材 a graceful figure
瘦削的身材 a lean figure
匀称的身材 a neat figure
丰满的身材 a plump figure

大腹便便的身材　a paunchy figure
细长的身材　a slender figure
苗条的身材　a slim figure
瘦小的身材　a slight figure
矮壮的身材　a stocky figure
高大的身材　a tall figure
优美健壮的身材　a superb figure
又胖又圆的身材　a full figure
笨拙的身材　an ungainly figure

“脸型”的常见英语表达：

圆圆的脸　a round face
椭圆的脸　an oval face
方脸　a square face
长脸　a long face
瘦削的脸　a thin/lean face
胖脸　a fleshy face
浮肿的脸　a puffy face
憔悴的面容　a haggard face
布满皱纹的脸　a wrinkled/lined face
长满粉刺的脸　a pimpled face
布满泪珠的脸　a tear-stained face
长满雀斑的脸　a freckled face
麻脸　a pock-marked face
眉清目秀的脸蛋　a finely-cut face
面目端正的脸　a regular face
丑脸　a disfigured face
妩媚的脸　a charming face
刮得精光的脸　a clean-shaved face
黝黑的面孔　a swarthy face
晒黑的脸　a sunburned face
秀丽的脸　a sweet face
铁板般的面孔　a stern face

“眼睛”的常见英语表达：

乌黑的眼睛　dark eyes
灰色的眼睛　gray eyes
绿色的眼睛　green eyes
蓝色的眼睛　blue eyes
深蓝色的眼睛　violet eyes
深棕色的眼睛　brown eyes
淡褐色的眼睛　hazel eyes
睁得圆圆的眼睛　wide-open eyes
鼓起来的眼睛　bulging eyes
深陷的眼睛　deep-set eyes
凹陷的眼睛　sunken eyes
斜眼的　cross-eyed
斜视眼　slant eyes
一只眼的　one-eyed
充满血丝的眼睛　bloodshot eyes

“睫毛”的常见英语表达：

细细的睫毛　thin eyelashes
浓密的睫毛　thick eyelashes
笔直的睫毛　strait eyelashes
短睫毛　short eyelashes
弯弯的睫毛　curved eyelashes

“鼻子”的常见英语表达：

鹰钩鼻子　an aquiline nose
扁鼻子　a flat nose
翘鼻子　a snub nose
笔直的鼻子　a straight nose

“眉毛”的常见英语表达：

浓眉　bushy eyebrows　　粗眉　shaggy eyebrows

弓形眉毛　arched eyebrows　　描画过的眉毛　penciled eyebrows

“额头”的常见英语表达：

宽大的额头　a broad forehead　　突起的额头　a domed forehead

高高的额头　a high forehead　　宽阔的额头　an open forehead

窄小的额头　a narrow forehead　　后塌的额头　a retreating forehead

“面颊”的常见英语表达：

红润的双颊　rosy cheeks　　丰满的双颊　chubby cheeks

苍白的双颊　pale cheeks　　粉红的双颊　pink cheeks

红光满面的双颊　ruddy cheeks　　深陷的双颊　hollow/sunken cheeks

刮得精光的脸颊　clean-shaven cheeks　　涂脂抹粉的脸颊　rouged cheeks

胡须满面的双颊　stubby cheeks　　布满皱纹的双颊　wrinkled cheeks

“下巴”的常见英语表达：

双下巴　a double chin　　尖尖的下巴　a pointed chin

圆圆的下巴　a round chin　　翘起的下巴　a protruding chin

描述“服饰”的常见英语表达：

潇洒的　smart　　邋遢的　scruffy

衣着华丽的　well-dressed　　随便的　casual

不显眼的　conservative　　优雅的　elegant

时髦的　fashionable　　文雅的　suave

不整洁的　untidy

关于人物的动作描写，能否写得生动形象、写得传神，重点在于动词的使用是否准确。选用动词一定要精准、贴切，切忌模糊宽泛或用词不当、词不达意。比如“He turned his horse around and galloped quickly home.”这一句中使用了 gallop 这个动词，其字典里的解释为：when a horse or similar animal gallops, it moves very fast and each stride includes a stage when all four feet are off the ground together，本意是指“（马等）飞奔，奔驰，疾驰”，也可以用来指人，表现出主人公策马奔腾、飞速赶回家的动作和心急如焚的心情。若是改为动词 go，虽然也表达了“返回家中、回家”的意思，但是就不如 gallop 生动形象，语言的表现力也弱了很多。再比如“He took his sword and swung it at the dog.”这一句中使用了动词 swing 来描写主人公挥剑杀死 Gelert 的动作。这个词在字典里的解释为：to try to hit sb/sth，就是“挥动某物朝……打去”的意思。使用 swing 这个动词可以形象地勾勒出主人公举起手中的剑并用力挥向 Gelert 的画面，表现出主人公痛失爱子的悲痛和对“杀死”自己儿子的 Gelert 的仇恨。若是改为 kill 这个动词，虽然也是“杀死、砍死、刺死”的意思，但是信息量就不那么丰富，也不够生动，无法给读者留下深刻的印象。再比如“Just as it was leaving, Mr Taylor rushed out and ran after it throwing ashtrays and vases.” 这句话中的rush一词充分表现出了珠宝店老板泰勒先生看到大量珠宝钻石被劫匪团伙抢走时的慌乱和试图阻止劫匪逃跑的急切心情,如果换成普通的动词词组get out就显得苍白许多。又比如,关于“出门去”这个动作,简单一句go/get out of door并不能刻画出一个人出门的方式和细节。如果是出门去上班,我们可以用leave for work;如果是赶时间、很匆忙地出门,我们可以说hurry away;如果是动作很快甚至飞奔而出,我们可以说rush out;而如果是刻意避免被人注意到而悄悄溜出门去,我们可以用slip/sneak out。这样用词准确的动作描写可以营造故事的紧张气氛或增强情节的画面感,使故事更加生动有趣、引人入胜。

语言描写中要避免使用过于笼统、宽泛、模糊的动词,而要尽量做到用词贴切。比如语言描写中“某人说……”这个表达,如果只是用Someone said...来表达的话,say这个动词就过于笼统了。如果是对别人说话后的补充,我们可以用Someone added...;如果是回答别人的提问,我们可以用Someone answered...; 如果是对某人的话作出的回应或者回复,我们可以用Someone replied...;如果是指出或强调某一问题,我们可以用Someone pointed out that...或Someone stressed/emphasized...;如果是小声说话,我们可以用Someone whispered...或Someone murmured...;如果是重复前面说过的话,我们可以使用Someone repeated...;如果是大声惊呼着喊出的话,我们可以用Someone exclaimed...;如果是笑着说的话,我们可以用Someone laughed...;如果是非常正式地宣布一件事情,我们可以说Someone announced...或Someone stated...;如果是对某一问题的解释,我们可以用Someone explained...或Someone clarified...。

关于人物情绪和心理感受方面的描写,我们可以直抒胸臆,直接进行描写,但是更高级的写法是“感时花溅泪,恨别鸟惊心”,即通过外在环境的衬托、人物语言动作的表现等来对人物的内心进行间接描写。比如如果描写悲伤,就不能只写悲伤,还可以写万物凋零、寒风刺骨、乌云蔽日,写“无边落木萧萧下”,写“杜鹃啼血猿哀鸣”。同理,除了直白的He is sad,还可以这样写:“He buried his face in his hands.”“With a heavy heart, he dragged his feet home, his shoulders drooping like a wilted flower in the desert.” 这些更有画面感的描写会使人物的心理刻画更加入木三分。

描写“高兴”的常见英语表达:

be wild with joy
to one's delight
amazed/proud and excited
be over the moon
be on cloud nine
be/feel on the top of the world
feel like floating in the ocean of happiness
feel as though having won a lottery
feel as happy as a king/clam

间接描写“高兴”的方法：

动作

jump with joy

clap one's hands

jump/leap/spring/bounce to one's feet

quicken one's pace/steps home spontaneously

trot home with little hops

dash out like a free bird

cheer/applaud for sb

give sb the thumbs-up

wave one's hands wildly/triumphantly

Delighted and thrilled, she trotted back home, humming and skipping like a bird in the forest.

Hard as she tried, her exciting voice betrayed her excitement.

神态

wear a radiant/proud/shining smile

grin from ear to ear

His face glowed/flushed/lit up with delight/pride.

Her eyes twinkled with excitement/joy/contentment.

My heart is as sweet as honey.

The smile flashed/spread across her face.

His lips curved into a bright/broad/brilliant smile/grin.

环境

At the sight of the sunrise, we felt as if on the top of the world.

With gentle breeze kissing her cheeks, she walked in the forest like a jolly elf.

The sunset was casting a glow over the village, the birds were tweeting merrily in the trees, and the grass were swaying happily in the wind as if sharing my joy.

Golden sunlight danced in her long hair and the children's laughter floated in the air.

描写“悲伤”的常见英语表达：

be filled with sadness

to one's dismay

grieved/upset and disappointed

can't hold back one's tears

be down in the dumps

be downcast

be under the weather

have the blues

feel like drowning in an ocean of sadness

feel as though their world had come crashing down

feel as miserable as a homeless dog

间接描写“悲伤”的方法：

动作

sob with sorrow

weep for sb

shake one's head

hang one's head in sorow

slump down in despair

bury one's face in one's hands

tremble with sorow

stumble and stagger blindly

sob uncontrollably/silently

Despite her best efforts to conceal it, her trembling voice betrayed her sadness.

神态

wear a sad/desperate/disappointed frown

a lump in his/her throat

unable to speak

be overcome with sadness

His face was clouded/darkened with sadness/disappointment.

His eyes were filled with tears/sorrow/hurt.

His heart is as heavy as a stone.

A tear slid down her cheek.

His lips trembled with sadness.

Tears were welling up in his eyes.

环境

The sky was overcast with dark clouds, and a cold wind blew, adding to the somber atmosphere.

The rain fell relentlessly, as if washing away the sadness in the air.

The leaves on the trees trembled in the wind, as if echoing the mournful cries of those in pain.

The silence was deafening, broken only by the sound of sobbing and the raindrops hitting the pavement.

The once-bright flowers now drooped, their colors faded, mirroring the sadness in everyone's heart.

The sun disappeared behind the thick clouds, leaving the world in a state of perpetual gloom.

（五）迁移创新

微场景 1:John 在音乐会上欣赏到了他最喜欢的乐队的表演。

As the band played their final song, John 1) __________ (情不自禁开心地跳了起来). Lisa, who was sitting next to him, looked at him in surprise and said, "Wow, you look like you're having the time of your life!" John replied, "I am! This band is amazing! They always manage to lift my spirits and make me feel alive."

微场景 2:生日派对上,孩子们兴奋地拆着礼物。

At the birthday party, the children were eagerly unwrapping their presents, 2) __________ (他们的眼中闪烁着期待和惊喜). 3) __________ (他们的脸上洋溢着喜悦和兴奋) as they discovered the surprises inside the wrapping paper. 4) __________ (微笑在他们的嘴角边荡开), radiating pure happiness and gratitude. The whole room was filled with the sounds of laughter and cheers, creating a joyous atmosphere.

微场景 3:比赛失利。

The player 5) __________ (羞愧地低下了头) after losing the game. Tears streamed down his face as he 6) __________ (悲伤地抽泣着). He felt as though 7) __________ (世界已经崩溃), and his dreams had been shattered. Despite the support of his teammates, he couldn't help but feel defeated.

参考答案:

1) couldn't contain his excitement and jumped with joy

2) their eyes sparkling with anticipation and amazement

3) Their faces lit up with joy and excitement

4) Smiles spread across their lips

5) hung his head in shame

6) sobbed with sorrow

7) his world had come crashing down

（六）作品舞台

学生作品 1

My mother is an ordinary woman, who is 1.58 meters tall. With kind appearance and good manners, she looks very admirable and graceful if you meet her. She has a pair of keen eyes which can speak. Whenever I encounter difficulties, her eyes will encourage me and help me cheer up. When I began learning to walk, my mother always lent me a hand and encouraged me to stand up while I fell down. As I finally threw myself into her arms, her eyes smiled with praise. After I entered school, my mother's eyes still encouraged me. Once I failed in my Chinese exam, my mother helped me find out the reasons instead of blaming me. Now I have grown up and my mother is always helping our neighbors or strangers, which makes her gain good honors in our village. Whenever somebody needs aids, she will give her hands as much as she can.

学生互评：

这篇描写妈妈的文章在描写妈妈的外貌时，非常鲜明地突出描写了妈妈的眼睛。不仅有客观描写，还有妈妈的眼睛带给"我"的主观感受，即对"我"的关爱和鼓励，写得非常传神。品质描写方面，则举了具体的事例来表明妈妈是一个特别善良、乐于助人的人。但是有一个语言错误："... my mother always lent me a hand and encouraged me to stand up while I fell down."这句话中的 while 应改为 when。

学生作品 2

I sat in my own seat, excited and grateful. After all the torture of writing the same essay for six times, I finally realized what Mr Smith actually intended me to do. Rather than a punishment, the essay assignment was designed to improve my writing skills and make me behave well. How ashamed I was of my bad attitude! I was so wrong that I didn't realize how lucky I was until then to have such a kind, patient and responsible teacher. I made up my mind to take my study seriously from then on and listen to Mr Smith carefully in class. I often share the lesson I learnt from this experience and the influence Mr Smith has on me. Without Mr Smith, I couldn't be what I am today.

教师点评：

文章使用了许多形容词来描写人物的心理活动，如 excited、grateful、ashamed、wrong、lucky。文中还使用了一些亮点词汇和句型，如 rather than, be designed to do..., not... until..., How... I was...等，体现了作者扎实的语言功底。名词性从句（what Mr Smith actually intended me to do）和虚拟语气（Without Mr Smith, I couldn't be what I am today.）的使用提升了写作档次，增加了文章的亮点。

二、新闻人物，意志品格

（一）类别解析

新闻人物报道是一种时效性比较强的文体，通过讲述人物的具体事迹来刻画人物形象、塑造和表现人物品格。新闻人物报道通常使用具体数据来描述事实，内容客观、准确。从语篇结构来看，新闻人物报道通常包括新闻标题、导语、正文、结尾这几部分，具备新闻报道的典型要素。新闻人物报道首先报道发生的重大新闻事件，与标题呼应，然后再详细报道其他相关的背景信息或人物经历，在结尾部分往往会升华总结人物的优秀品格或激励读者思考对自身的启示。

（二）精研文本

译林版新教材必修第三册第四单元 Reading 部分的文本 *Chinese Scientist Wins* 2015 *Nobel Prize* 是一篇新闻人物报道，内容围绕中国第一位获得诺贝尔奖的女科学家屠呦呦展开。文章的文体特征非常明显，有标题、记者名字、报道时间，内容分为三部分：导语部分（An exciting news report）、人物经历（A rewarding journey）和取得成就（A sincere tribute）。

文章开篇在第一段的导语中对中国科学家屠呦呦获得诺贝尔奖的新闻事件进行了简要报道，包括获奖的时间、原因以及重大意义。导语部分体现了这篇新闻人物报道的主要内容（who，what，why，when，where）。接下来第二部分详细报道了屠呦呦带领科研团队研发青蒿素的过程。文章通过大量数字，比如 collected 2000 traditional Chinese medicine recipes、an over 1600-year-old text、after 190 failures 等，描绘了屠呦呦团队在研发青蒿素过程中遇到的各种困难和为此所付出的巨大努力，体现出科学家们为科学献身的敬业精神和坚忍不拔的意志。

（三）课例展示

教材：人教版新教材选择性必修第一册第一单元 Reading and Thinking 部分的文本 *Tu Youyou Awarded Nobel Prize*

文本分析：本课依据单元主题意义探究和学习活动观等理念，首先从分析语篇类型入手，以新闻六要素为基础形成问题链，引导学生探索文本中的事实类信息，开展基于语篇的阅读教学；随后，深入探究语篇内容，分析人物品质及其科学精神，引导学生全面理解文章内涵；最后，超越语篇，引导学生形成自己的观点并合理表达，提升其批判性思维及创新能力。本课旨在通过以上环节提升学生的阅读理解能力，培养学生的科学素养和人文精神。

教学目标)))

1. 识别语篇体裁，获取语篇中的事实类信息；
2. 描述并阐释青蒿素的发现过程，分析屠呦呦及其团队的人物品质及科学精神；
3. 分析和判断屠呦呦及其团队成功的原因；
4. 联系实际，总结学习语篇对学生的启示。

教学重点)))

1. 引导学生利用流程图梳理和概括屠呦呦的生平和发现青蒿素的主要过程，并分析和总结屠呦呦及其团队的品质及科学精神；

2. 引导学生分析和探讨屠呦呦成功的原因，表达屠呦呦发现青蒿素并获得诺贝尔奖这一事件对自己的启示。

教学步骤)))

Activity 1：Lead-in

Introduce the main character of the text using a famous saying from *Book of Songs*.

引出本堂课的主要人物，为阅读文本做好铺垫。

Activity 2：Read for text type

Lead students to judge and analyse the text type, structure and language features through the following questions.

1. Where would you most likely find this passage?

2. Passages like this are most often written in ________ and ________.

3. If you were the journalist, what aspects would you write about in a news report?

Then, lead students to be aware of the six elements of a news report.

教师通过引导学生分析文本，培养学生辨识语篇类型及语言特点的能力，逐步形成语篇意识，并引导学生说出新闻六要素，为下一项阅读活动做好准备。学生通过阅读判断出这篇文章是一篇报纸上的新闻人物报道。学生观察文本，发现文本由标题、日期、导语、正文主体和结尾几个部分构成。这样的新闻人物报道往往使用第三人称进行叙述，主动语态和被动语态兼有，涵盖大量事实陈述。然后，教师结合文本，引导学生用思维导图列出新闻报道的六要素：who, what, why, when, where, how。

Activity 3：Read for information

Based on the mind map of the six elements of a news report provided by students, lead students to read the text and extract factual and detailed information from the text, especially Tu's life experience and the whole process of discovering artemisinin. After that, lead students to describe Tu and her team's great qualities and scientific spirit.

利用思维导图及流程图，引导学生了解语篇的核心内容，即屠呦呦团队发现青蒿素的过程。从试验前、试验中、试验后三个阶段来梳理信息，并引导学生关注其中的关键动词：examined、evaluated、found、tested、tried、used、tested、became，体会研究团队的辛苦钻研和投身医学的敬业精神，学会用批判性思维看待人与事，建立向具有优秀品质的人物学习的意识。

Activity 4：Read for reasons

Lead students to read the text again and find out the reasons why Tu and her team succeeded.

通过深入阅读语篇，分析讨论文本中的数字，对屠呦呦成功的原因形成正确认识。分析归纳科学家屠呦呦具备的品质：professional、committed、patient、selfless。

Activity 5：Voice your ideas

Lead students to think about the significance of the discovery for which Tu was awarded the Nobel Prize. Provide tips for students to discuss with their group members：What effects does it have on the whole world? On China? On us?

最后这一环节引导学生探究主题意义并形成正确的理解，从而深刻理解我国传统中医药对人类健康和世界发展的贡献，有助于学生增强国家认同，坚定文化自信，不仅有利于培养学生的文化意识，还能引导学生思考成长的意义与未来努力的方向。

板书设计

Reading and Thinking

Tu Youyou Awarded Nobel Prize

a news report：objective，accurate，convincing

who，what，why，when，where，how

descriptions provided by students in class

（四）技巧归纳

新闻人物报道具有新闻性，是对事实的报道。从结构方面来讲，新闻人物报道符合新闻的体裁特点，通常由标题、导语、人物背景介绍、人物事迹或成就、人物评价或思考感悟等构成。从语言方面来讲，新闻人物报道讲述人物的人生故事或伟大成就时，要有细节描写，要尽可能详细深入地讲述人物的具体事迹，同时运用多种表现手法，如记叙、议论、抒情等来刻画人物形象，塑造和表现人物品格。除了常见的语言描写、动作描写、心理描写，新闻人物报道还可以通过环境描写来衬托人物形象，以及通过描写矛盾冲突来刻画人物形象，因为在面对矛盾时的思考、选择、行为、态度等最容易显露人物的性格特征。语言生动准确，文章才会富有感染力，人物塑造才会充实饱满，才能打动读者，引起共鸣或引人深思，从而体现新闻报道的舆论引导作用。同时也要注意，虽然可以增加生动有趣的情节使人物及故事更加丰富、具备可读性，但新闻报道本质上要以真实报道为中心，不能随意夸大、添加、编造事实。从内容方面来讲，要注意并非所有第一手的新闻素材都可以写进报道，还需经过分析、筛选、提炼和加工，选取其中贴近时代主题、有助于体现新闻人物品格的相关内容。

(五)迁移创新

1. 假如你是学校英语报的一名记者,请根据所给提示写一篇报道,介绍考古学家樊锦诗,并发表在学校英语报上。

注意:(1)词数 80 左右;

(2)可以适当增加细节,以使行文连贯。

出生年月	1938 年 7 月
主要贡献	建立"数字敦煌",编写了许多与敦煌莫高窟相关的书籍,为敦煌莫高窟的保护做出了巨大贡献
评价	2019 年 9 月,被授予"文物保护杰出贡献者"国家荣誉称号 2020 年,被评为"感动中国"人物之一

参考词汇:文物保护杰出贡献者　outstanding contributor to cultural relics protection

国家荣誉称号　national honorary title

2. 为了保护城市中的文化遗产,有很多平凡的普通人在默默地努力着,贡献自己的力量。请根据以下表格中的采访笔记撰写一篇新闻人物报道。

Chen Lei, Wuhan
• senior teacher • takes photos of old buildings • wants to preserve cultural heritage • interviews old people • writes about the buildings • visits schools to tell students about…

(六)作品舞台

学生作品 1

Born in July 1938, Fan Jinshi is an archaeologist and works in Dunhuang, Northwest China's Gansu Province. Fan Jinshi has buried her head in the study of ancient heritage. She has established the "Digital Dunhuang", which prevents Dunhuang's cultural heritage from disappearing. She has written many books about the Mogao Caves, which had a great influence on the protection of the Mogao Caves. Fan Jinshi has contributed greatly to the protection of

Dunhuang's cultural relics. In September 2019, she was given the national honorary title of "Outstanding Contributor to Cultural Relics Protection". In 2020, she was honored as one of the people "Moving China".

教师点评：

文章内容要点完整，表达准确有条理。但是从新闻人物报道的结构来讲，首先需要包括标题、导语和正文部分，才能称得上是一篇新闻报道。建议增加新闻标题，并用一句话高度概括人物取得的主要成就，作为报道的导语部分，然后再展开叙述人物的生平和所作出的贡献。

学生作品2

Chen Lei is a senior teacher who takes photos of old buildings in Wuhan in order to preserve the city's cultural heritage. Every day, Chen Lei takes his camera and takes photos of old buildings in Wuhan that can best represent the history of the city. Besides, he also interviews old people who have witnessed the change of the street scenes and writes articles for local newspapers so that more people can know about the stories of the old buildings. In his spare time, he often visits schools to tell students about what happened to the old buildings in the past, which makes them realize how important the buildings are and that we should take action to protect them. Neither people nor buildings last forever, but Chen Lei's photos can help us remember them.

学生互评：

这篇文章开头有导语句，正文部分详细讲述了人物所做的事情和其意义，令读者意识到保护老建筑需要每一个人的努力。语言方面，文章使用了较多的复合句，比如用了大量的定语从句，对人物事迹进行了准确而详细的描述。

三、人物传记，楷模榜样

（一）类别解析

人物传记是记录人物生平事迹的一种文体，因撰写者的不同可以分为自传和他传，因语言风格不同可分为一般性传记和文学性传记。一般性传记以记述人物生平、经历等事实为主，而文学性传记会使用多种文学写作手段和形象化的写作技巧来描述人物的生活、性格、思想感情等，不仅具有史料价值，更追求文学价值。人物传记可以写人物整个人生的经历，也可以只写其中某一段，比如童年时期或求学时期的经历。除了记述人物的主要经历以外，人物传记还可以对人物进行简要的评价，用议论性的语言刻画人物。人物传记通常按时间顺序介绍人物的一生，包括成长经历、接受教育情况、兴趣爱好、性格品质、工作经历、感人事迹、突出成绩、伟大成就等。

（二）精研文本

人教版新教材必修第三册第二单元中 Reading and Thinking 板块的文本 *Mother of Ten Thousand Babies* 是一篇人物传记，以第三人称和一般过去时叙述了林巧稚的一生。第一部分引用人物原话，引入文章主题；第二部分按照时间顺序叙述林巧稚在面临人生几个重要选择时做出的决定；第三部分描写人物成就。文章根据时间顺序和历史事件发生的先后顺序叙述了林巧稚的生平事迹，着重描写了她在一生中曾面临的艰难的人生抉择：是遵循中国传统道德观念结婚成家，还是追寻医学梦？是留在条件优厚的异国发展，还是回到苦难深重的祖国效力？是保全生命放弃悬壶济世，还是开办诊所救国救民？是选择拥有地位和家庭，还是为了中国的无数家庭而献身工作？文章通过 instead of、be more interested in、-ing 作状语和宾语补足语等词组和方式生动细致地描写了人物的选择，并多次引用了林巧稚原话的英语译文，真实而有说服力，深入刻画了她的高贵品质。在面临人生的重大抉择时，林巧稚选择将个人发展与国家发展和社会需要结合，她所做出的抉择无不反映了她坚定的信念、美好的心灵、高度的职业责任感和奉献精神。通过林巧稚人生道路上遇到的选择困境及她做出的人生选择和带来的影响，文章展现了人物值得赞颂的美德，从而使学生理解林巧稚每次人生重大抉择背后体现的人生观，呼应单元主题在本篇文章中的体现：Learn to make choices in life，引导学生思考人生中的重大抉择及原因，并结合生活实际阐述如何在面对人生机遇时做出体现家国情怀和中华美德的人生选择。

外研版新教材必修第三册第二单元的单元主题语境是“人与社会”，涉及的主题是“优秀品行与社会责任感”。Developing Ideas 板块中的 *The Power of Good* 一文的语篇类型为人物传记，介绍了 Nicholas Winton 的生平和伟大事迹。Winton 出生于 20 世纪初，当时犹太人遭到纳粹的迫害，纷纷逃离德国。Winton 冒着巨大的风险帮助犹太人摆脱纳粹的追捕，将大批犹太儿童送到安全地区，并想方设法筹集资金为犹太儿童提供食宿。截至 1939 年 8 月，Winton 累计救助了 669 名犹太儿童，但是直到 1988 年他的妻子向报纸公布了他的日记，大众才知道他在过去几十年中为保护犹太儿童所做的一切。文章以时间顺序为线索，用第三人称叙述了 Winton 伟大的一生，展现了人物不畏艰难险阻、坚持善行、关爱弱势群体的国际人道主义精神。文章以犹太儿童被送上火车转移到安全地方的情境开篇，点明了人物 Winton 的主要事迹。第二部分是 Winton 的个人简介，包括他的出生年月、家庭背景、早年工作经历。第三部分是文章的重点，着重叙述了 1938 年 Winton 在布拉格时和二战期间从英国皇家空军退役并加入国际组织后对犹太儿童的救助，展现了 Winton 的人生经历：目睹犹太人的苦难——决定实施救助——募捐并倾囊相助——为犹太儿童寻找住所——施行善举后未被大众知晓。最后三段列出了 Winton 所获得的认可和荣誉，以及 Winton 在 106 岁去世时作者对人物的评价：As the Chinese saying goes, “A kind-hearted person lives a long life.”

（三）课例展示

教材：人教版新教材选择性必修第一册第五单元 Reading and Thinking 板块的文本 *A Pioneer for All People*

文本分析：本单元的主题意义为深度思考农业发展对社会民生、国家建设乃至世界和平的重大意义，联系生活实际提出解决饥饿问题的可行方案，树立正确的价值观和事业观，将个人追求和理想事业等规划与国家和社会的发展需求相结合。本节课的整体教学思路是以两个主线问题（How & Why）为引领，依托多重探究活动，引导学生深入研读文本，通过与教材对话、与教师对话、与同伴对话、与作者对话，逐步解构文本内容，逐层探究主题意义。教学主环节从标题出发，最终回归标题，形成一个自然的主题探究逻辑闭环，学生也能实现从文本内容到文本主题最终到思维提升的思维逻辑闭环，实现深度学习。首先，借助标题和图片预测文本内容，激活已知，进入文本主题；接着，利用阅读策略快速获取文本段落大意，厘清文本内容框架；然后，继续深入语篇，聚焦标题，从而生成主线问题，获取并梳理关于袁隆平的生平和成就的信息（How），总结使他成为先驱的美好品质（Why）；最后，在读后的分析评价环节中，基于袁隆平的个人事迹和优秀品质，深度解读标题内涵，结合所学所思进行输出。

教学目标

1. 借助标题和图片预测文本内容，利用阅读策略快速获取文本段落大意，厘清文本内容框架；

2. 深入阅读文本，获取并梳理关于袁隆平的生平和成就的信息（How），分析使他成为先驱的优秀品质（Why）；

3. 基于袁隆平的个人事迹和优秀品质，深度解读标题内涵，结合所学所思进行创意表达。

教学重点

1. 深入阅读文本，分析使袁隆平成为全人类先驱的优秀品质；

2. 通过分享主人公事迹和优秀品质带来的感悟和启示，激发学生对农业科学家的崇敬之情，提升对农业发展的认识，同时做到语言、思维和文化的融合。

教学步骤

Activity 1：Lead-in（激活已知，进入文本主题）

Invite students to read a poem about Yuan Longping together and ask, "What do you know about Yuan?" Students will read a poem *You Love the Land Entirely* and share what they know about Yuan. This step is to activate the background knowledge.

通过诗歌引入主题，自然过渡到本课的话题和核心人物，激发学生的已有认知和学习兴趣，并培养口头表达能力。

Activity 2：Pre-reading（聚焦标题，生成主线问题）

Ask students to look at the title and pictures, and predict what they may read from the passage. Students will look at the title and pictures and put forward some questions：what/why/how/achievements/difficulties. This step is to let students predict the content.

引导学生针对标题和图片进行自主解读和自主提问，提出涵盖两个主线问题的相关问题，既形成阅读期待，保证了阅读过程的指向性和系统性，提高了自主阅读的效率，也能使信息结构化，为后续深度解读文本、深挖两条主线搭建好探究的“脚手架”，同时也培养了学生的逻辑推理和分析判断能力。

Activity 3：While-reading（逐层阅读，探究主题意义）

Guide students to skim the passage and summarize the main idea of each part. Students will skim the passage and share their ideas. This step is to let students identify the structure of the text.

要求学生快速浏览全文，总结文章各部分大意，帮助学生实现整体阅读，为后续深度解读文本和主题做铺垫，由此培养学生归纳、总结文本重点内容和解构文本框架的能力。

Activity 4：Analyzing key information（How）（聚焦事件，获取文本内容）

Guide students to read the whole passage and find out as much evidence as possible to prove “How did Yuan become a pioneer for all people?” Students will read and underline key information（verbs）and then share it with the whole class.

本环节聚焦文章的内容层面，给学生充分的时间去阅读、理解文章，引导学生以主线问题 How（明线）为抓手，培养学生自主学习、分析文本的能力。然后，通过小组讨论和分享，用结构图梳理袁隆平成为先驱者的历程，使袁隆平的人物形象更加丰满，帮助学生较为详细地把握文章细节，从而提升学生获取信息的能力和锻炼学生的综合语言表达能力。

Activity 5：Summarizing good qualities（Why）（归纳品质，探知人物精神）

Guide students to discuss in groups and use adjectives to summarize Yuan's personalities with supporting evidence, and to understand “Why is he called a pioneer for all people?” Students will work in groups, writing adjectives on the given cards and giving supporting evidence with complete sentences by referring to possible sentence patterns.

在梳理袁隆平成为先驱者历程的基础上，引导学生以主线问题 Why（暗线）为抓手，讨论分析其被称为“先驱者”的原因，总结袁隆平的优秀品质和高尚精神，并结合文本进行描述和阐释,促进优质产出和结构化知识的形成,为后续环节做铺垫。本活动旨在提升学生处理信息的能力,锻炼学生分析问题、提炼观点的能力,培养学生的批判性思维,并提升团队合作能力。

Activity 6: Appreciating the title & the writing technique (回归标题,深化文本主题)

Guide students to reread the title and ask "How do you understand 'all people' according to the passage?". Students will read and find other identities of Yuan in the passage.

引导学生结合典型事件和人物品质回看标题,更好地理解 Yuan is "a pioneer from all people and for all people"的深刻内涵,提升学生的语言运用能力,实现对语言知识的深度加工,让学生在体悟人物精神的同时深化文本主题。本活动旨在培养学生分析信息、解构文本的能力,以及培养学生的批判性思维。

Activity 7: Post-reading (分析评价,重塑思维价值)

Ask students to think, "What have you learnt from Yuan?" Students will think about the question and share their ideas in class. This step is to consolidate what they have learnt and transfer new knowledge.

通过分享学习袁隆平故事的感悟,促进学生对语篇主题内容和意义的吸收和内化,同时融入情感教育,引发学生对人生的积极思考,使其在对自我的反思中逐步修正、重构自身的价值观,并将其内化为个人的意志和品行,实现从"人与社会"到"人与自我"的主题迁移,培养积极的价值观。

Activity 8: Assignments

Option 1: Make a poster with the title *My Hero—Dr. Yuan*.

Option 2: Write a short passage about your favorite scientist.

(四)技巧归纳

人物传记最重要的就是真实、生动。记录人物成长经历或伟大事迹时一定要以事实为基础,切不可编造,否则就失去了可信度,丧失了史料价值。同时,人物传记不同于人物简介,它不仅仅是事实的简单罗列,还要通过生动的语言刻画出人物的典型形象。人物传记的内容也要有所取舍,不必事无巨细、面面俱到地记录人物的一生,而要精心选取有利于凸显人物形象的人生片段和典型经历进行描写。比如外研版新教材必修第三册第三单元中的 *The Power of Good* 一文,并没有全面记述人物 Nicholas Winton 的生平,而是着重介绍了他如何在二战期间在纳粹统治下解救犹太儿童的这一部分经历,突出了人物善良助人的可贵品质。

（五）迁移创新

回想你最崇拜的一位科学家、伟人或历史人物，为他/她撰写一篇人物传记，简要叙述其人物生平、取得的成就和对你所产生的影响。

（六）作品舞台

学生作品 1

Dr. Zhong Nanshan was born in October 1936 in Nanjing, Jiangsu Province. He is one of the famous medical scientists in the 21st century. He studied at Guangdong Experimental High School in 1953 and graduated from Beijing Medical College in 1960. In the first Chinese National Games, Zhong Nanshan got the championship of the men's 400 m Hurdles and set up a national record at that time. In the spring of 2003, the SARS epidemic broke out in China and across the globe. Zhong Nanshan not only led but also took an active part in the battle against SARS. At that time, no one really knew much about SARS and most people had no natural defenses against the disease. Dangerous as it was, Zhong Nanshan worked hard day and night treating the patients. Through their hard work for several months, Zhong Nanshan and his workmates achieved remarkable results. Soon the SARS epidemic was stopped in its track. Zhong Nanshan was awarded one of the top ten people "Moving China" in 2004. He has been working in the medical field for over 60 years. He is a good doctor in the countrymen's eyes and respected by all the people in China.

教师点评：

文章语言流畅，内容丰富充实，涵盖了钟南山的成长经历、接受教育情况、兴趣特长、工作经历、突出成就等，从人物传记的结构方面来讲，很好地完成了写作任务。但是其中关于钟南山参加跨栏项目全国夺冠的经历和文章其他部分的内容联系不大，略显突兀，建议删去或改为生活中能够反映人物品格和特点的其他事迹。

学生作品 2

Zhang Guimei, born in 1957 in Mudanjiang City, Heilongjiang Province, works in a middle school in Huaping County, Yunnan Province, in a multi-ethnic mountainous area. In her 29 years of work, she has been awarded numerous honors, and the one she cherishes most is the common title: a people's teacher. As a teacher, Zhang loves the children as if they were her own. She says, "Love is the key for heart-to-heart communication between teachers and students." Since all her students come from minority groups and their cultural level is lower than average, she has to work harder for longer hours to design teaching methods that can arouse their motivation to learn. Her efforts are well rewarded with their good results in public examinations. Despite illness and pain, which torture her every day, Zhang continues her work and donates most of the money she earns to poor children in the countryside. She says,"My life is in my teaching."

学生互评:

文章主要写了张桂梅为华坪教育做出的巨大贡献和伟大牺牲,但是作为人物传记,没有写到人物的成长经历。语言上的特点是引用了人物的原话,显得真实又生动。

第二节　介绍地点

地点介绍通常包括以下几方面内容。

地理位置:介绍该地的大致位置,包括所在国家、省/州、城市等。

例如:The Grand Canyon is located in the state of Arizona in the southwestern United States.

科罗拉多大峡谷位于美国西南部的亚利桑那州。

历史文化:介绍该地的历史文化背景,包括历史发展、重要事件、文化地标等。

例如:Beijing, the capital city of China, has a history of over 3,000 years and is home to numerous cultural landmarks such as the Forbidden City and the Great Wall.

北京,中国的首都,有着3000多年的历史,是紫禁城和长城等众多文化地标的所在地。

自然风光:介绍该地的自然风光,包括自然景观、地形地貌、气候环境等。

例如:The Niagara Falls, located on the Niagara River on the border of Canada and the United States, is one of the most famous natural wonders in the world.

尼亚加拉大瀑布位于加拿大和美国交界处的尼亚加拉河畔,是世界上最著名的自然奇观之一。

名胜古迹:介绍该地的著名景点、地标建筑、历史遗迹等。

例如:Paris, the capital city of France, is famous for its iconic landmarks such as the Eiffel Tower, the Louvre Museum, and Notre-Dame Cathedral.

法国首都巴黎以其标志性的建筑闻名,比如埃菲尔铁塔、卢浮宫博物馆和巴黎圣母院。

饮食文化:介绍该地的特色饮食文化。

例如:Tokyo is known for its diverse culinary scene, with popular dishes including sushi, ramen, and tempura.

东京以其多样化的烹饪场景而闻名,有很多受欢迎的菜肴,包括寿司、拉面和天妇罗。

除了以上内容,在介绍地点的时候也有很多不同的写作手法可以使用,下面我们详细介绍其中比较常见的几种。

一、五感写作法

（一）类别解析

介绍一个地点，可以从视觉、听觉、嗅觉、触觉、味觉、联想、回忆等方面进行多方位立体描写。细致的描写可以使所介绍的地点显得更加生动、立体，尤其是在描写中结合联想和回忆，将自身感受和美丽的景致融为一体，更能突出地点的特色，给人留下鲜明的印象。

（二）精研文本

新剑桥第四册第十二单元 Read and Listen 板块有三篇文本，分别介绍了“两河交汇（the Meeting of the Waters）”“红杉森林（Muir Woods）”和“艾尔斯岩（Ayers Rock）”。虽然三篇文本分别是小说、旅游博客和旅游指南，但是其中也使用了“五感写作法”，并重点描述了视觉、听觉和触觉，具体见下表。

视觉（Sight）	听觉（Sound）	触觉（Touch）
1. … as it crawled along the muddy brown waters of the Amazon. 2. … there was a line in the water—on one side, the brown water… and on the other, water that was as black as night. 3. … Uluru changes colour between shades of fiery red, delicate mauve, blue, pink and brown…	… the crew members began to wave and to call him.	1. The heat and the mosquitoes had become almost too much for them to bear. 2. … rainfall creates a silver veil over the entire rock.

两河交汇位于巴西马瑙斯市东部，尼格罗河和索里芒斯河在这里交汇之后并行不悖，形成一种奇特的景观。尼格罗河的茶黑色河水和富含泥沙的咖啡色的索里芒斯河河水在这里交汇。交汇之后，两条河流在同一河道中并肩而行几公里。索里芒斯河水温较低，密度更高，流速也较快；而尼格罗河水温较高，流速较慢。两条河流之间形成一条非常明显的边界。并行几公里之后，在巨大的漩涡和急流的作用下，两条河流最终混合在一起，合并成为亚马孙河下游。由于其最重要的特色就是两条颜色不同的河流并行，所以作者把描述重点放在了视觉上。同理，澳大利亚艾尔斯岩（又名“乌鲁鲁巨石”）随着太阳位置的变化，颜色会分别呈现出火红色、淡紫色、蓝色、粉红色和棕色，所以作者把描述重点也放在了视觉上。

人教版新教材选择性必修第一册第三单元 Reading and Thinking 板块的文章 *Sarek*

National Park—Europe's Hidden Natural Treasure 介绍了位于欧洲的萨勒克国家公园。语篇以第一人称视角,充分使用"五感写作法"带领读者体验一位徒步独行者的经历,与作者一起感受和体验萨勒克国家公园,具体见下表。

视觉(**Sight**)	1. Even though the sun is brightly shining, telling whether it is morning or night is impossible. 2. Spreading out before me, branches of the Rapa River flow through the valley below. 3. At the far side of the valley, an ancient Sami cottage is visible. Close by, there are a few reindeer feeding on grass.
嗅觉(**Smell**)	Here I am, alone under this broad sky, breathing the fresh air, and enjoying this great adventure.
味觉(**Taste**)	For example, this morning my breakfast is flat bread warmed over a fire, dried reindeer meat, and some sweet and sour berries that I found growing near my tent.
听觉(**Sound**)	I wake up to the sound of the wind buffeting the cloth of my tent.
触觉(**Touch**)	Since I must carry all of my food and supplies with me, my bag weighs about 30 kilograms. If today is anything like yesterday, it will be full of sweat and hard work as I hike over this difficult land to my destination on the other side of the valley.

教师可以用板书或演示文稿进行展示,并让学生说说自己的感受,体会这些描述在游记类语篇中的作用,从而引导学生在描述地点时注意类似的角度,学习通过细致的描写来增加文章的感染力。

(三)课例展示

教材:人教版新教材必修第二册第四单元 Reading for Writing 板块的文本 *Beautiful Ireland and Its Traditions*

文本分析:文本是一篇景物描写。作者从旅行者的角度,将爱尔兰乡村的景致、自身感受与当地的风土人情融为一体,内容丰富,语言优美,短小精悍。作者生动地描述了乡村美景和风土人情,在视觉、嗅觉、味觉、听觉和触觉等方面给读者带来了直观的感受。

教学目标)))

1. 分析文本结构,了解语言特色;

2. 赏析文中所使用的"五感写作法";

3. 用"五感写作法"描述一个地方。

教学步骤)))

Activity 1: Lead-in

通过谈论自己最近去过的旅游景点来激发学生的兴趣,引出语篇主题。

Activity 2: Fast reading

让学生带着下面的问题进行快速阅读。

What's the main idea of the passage?

A. The beautiful scenery of Ireland.

B. The history of Ireland.

C. The beautiful scenery and traditions of Ireland.

D. The customs of Ireland.

参考答案:C。

Activity 3: Careful reading

让学生带着下列问题仔细阅读文本。

1) What makes the Irish countryside exciting and inspiring?

2) What are the best ways to experience some Irish traditions and cultures?

3) What is the meaning of "breathe in the sweet scent of fresh flowers while birds greet the new day with their morning song"?

4) What are the best ways to experience Chinese traditions and customs?

参考答案:

1) Its beauty and how it offers something for all the scenes.

2) By stopping by a village pub and relaxing with a drink and traditional meal while listening to music and watching dancing.

3) It means to not just smell but also breathe in the smell of fresh flowers early in the morning as the birds sing their first song of the new day.

4) By traveling to different places and using all your senses to experience everything and by interacting with local people.

在描写动作时,除了精准使用动词和动作链,还可以从五感角度加上动作描写、场景描写、情绪描写,从而构建一个具体化的动作面。学生可以从视觉、嗅觉、味觉、听觉、触觉等多角度去感知,在脑海中勾勒出生动形象的画面。那么五感是什么呢?五感的常规定义如下:

Sight—what you see with your eyes; details of surroundings and people that you can observe with your eyes.

Smell—what you smell with your nose; the scents and even the odors of the environment.

Taste—what you taste with your tongue/what you experience with your lips.

Sound—what you hear with your ears; sounds in the environment that you are in.

Touch—there are two categories of touch:

(1) how you feel, the emotions you experience in a situation.

(2) the texture of objects that you touch, which is the physical contact with objects/people.

从定义中我们可以看出，Sight(视觉)是指我们的眼睛所看到的；Smell(嗅觉)指鼻子闻到的气味；Taste(味觉)指舌头或嘴唇尝到的味道；Sound(听觉)是指耳朵所听到的；Touch(触觉)分为两个方面，一种为在特定情境中的感受，另一种是接触物体的感觉。

接下来，让学生填写表格，学习如何利用"五感写作法"进行地点描写。

视觉(Sight)	嗅觉(Smell)	味觉(Taste)	听觉(Sound)	触觉(Touch)

Activity 4: Exercise

分析下文中的"五感写作法"。

The Enchanting Serenity of the Ancient Forest

Tucked away from the hustle and bustle of the city lies an ancient forest, a sanctuary where nature's symphony plays in perfect harmony. As I step beneath the verdant canopy, the first sensation that greets me is the crisp, fresh air that fills my lungs, invigorating my spirit with each breath. The scent of damp earth and the subtle fragrance of blossoming wildflowers awaken my olfactory senses, transporting me to a world where time seems to stand still.

Visually, the forest is a feast for the eyes. Dappled sunlight filters through the dense foliage overhead, casting a mosaic of light and shadow on the forest floor. The towering trees, with their gnarled trunks and outstretched branches, stand as silent sentinels, their green leaves rustling in a gentle breeze. The vibrant hues of ferns and mosses create a tapestry of emerald, while the occasional flash of color from a bird or butterfly adds a touch of whimsy to the scene.

The sounds of the forest are as mesmerizing as the sights. The gentle murmur of the nearby stream, the rustling of leaves, and the distant hoot of an owl all weave together into a tranquil lullaby. The occasional chirping of birds and the soft patter of raindrops on leaves create a soothing rhythm that resonates with the heart. At times, the forest falls into a profound silence, a silence so deep that it becomes a sound in itself, a testament to the peace that nature bestows.

As I continue my stroll, the tactile sensations of the forest become more pronounced. The rough bark of the trees contrasts with the soft carpet of pine needles and fallen leaves beneath my feet. The coolness of the forest floor seeps through my shoes, a refreshing contrast to the warmth of the sunlight that dapples my skin. I reach out to touch the velvety petals of a wildflower, and its delicate texture is a gentle reminder of the forest's delicate balance.

The taste of the forest is more subtle, revealed through the occasional wild berry that dots the understory. The sweet, tangy flavor of a ripe raspberry or the slightly tart juice of a blackberry burst in my mouth, a wild treat that adds a layer of sensory delight to my forest experience.

In this ancient forest, each of my senses is awakened and captivated. The sights, sounds, smells, tastes, and textures create an unforgettable mosaic of experiences that speak to the soul. Here, in the heart of nature, I find a peace that transcends the noise of the modern world, a place where the ancient rhythms of the earth continue to pulse, reminding me of the enduring beauty of our natural world.

视觉 (**Sight**)	嗅觉 (**Smell**)	味觉 (**Taste**)	听觉 (**Sound**)	触觉 (**Touch**)

参考答案：

视觉（Sight）	嗅觉（Smell）	味觉（Taste）	听觉（Sound）	触觉（Touch）
Para. 2: Dappled sunlight filters through the dense foliage overhead（斑驳的阳光透过头顶浓密的树叶滤进来）; The vibrant hues of ferns and mosses create a tapestry of emerald（蕨类植物和苔藓的鲜艳色彩创造了一幅翠绿色的挂毯）	Para. 1: The scent of damp earth and the subtle fragrance of blossoming wildflowers（潮湿土壤的气息和盛开野花的淡淡香味）	Para. 5: the occasional wild berry that dots the understory（偶尔点缀在下层植被中的野生浆果）; The sweet, tangy flavor of a ripe raspberry or the slightly tart juice of a blackberry（成熟覆盆子的甜酸味或黑莓的微酸汁液）	Para. 3: The gentle murmur of the nearby stream（附近溪流的轻柔低语）; the distant hoot of an owl（远处猫头鹰的叫声）	Para. 4: The rough bark of the trees（树木粗糙的树皮）; the soft carpet of pine needles and fallen leaves beneath my feet（脚下松针和落叶铺成的柔软地毯）; The coolness of the forest floor seeps through my shoes（森林地面的凉爽透过我的鞋子渗透进来）
这些视觉细节使读者能够想象出森林的景象。	这些描述唤醒了读者的嗅觉。	这些味觉体验为森林的描写增添了一层感官享受。	这些声音构成了森林的交响乐。	这些触觉体验让读者感受到森林的物理特性。
通过这些详细的感官描写，文章创造了一个多维度的森林体验，让读者仿佛置身于这片古老的森林之中。				

作业：用“五感写作法”描写一个公园。

参考答案：

In the heart of the city lies a tranquil park, a sanctuary for the senses. The visual tapestry is a feast with lush green lawns, vibrant flower beds, and the azure sky reflected in the still pond. The sweet scent of blooming jasmine teases the nose, while the rustling of leaves and the gentle trickling of the fountain serenade the ears. The softness of the grass beneath my feet and the coolness of the pond water on my skin are a tactile delight. And on a warm summer day, the taste of a ripe, sun-warmed berry from the park's orchard is the perfect sweet finale to this symphony of sensations. This park is a haven where the soul finds peace amidst the urban bustle.

分析：

Sight：lush green lawns，vibrant flower beds，and the azure sky reflected in the still pond（郁郁葱葱的绿色草坪、生机勃勃的花坛和平静池塘中映照出的蔚蓝天空）

这些视觉元素为读者描绘了一个生动而宁静的场景，让读者能够想象公园的色彩和美丽。

Smell：The sweet scent of blooming jasmine（盛开的茉莉花的甜美香气）

这一细节激发了读者的嗅觉，为公园增添了香气，让读者能够想象在公园游玩时可能闻到的香气。

Taste：the taste of a ripe，sun-warmed berry（成熟的、被阳光温暖的浆果的味道）

这一感官细节激发了读者的味觉，为公园的整体体验增添了一种愉快而清新的元素。

Sound：the rustling of leaves（树叶的沙沙作响声）

the gentle trickling of the fountain（喷泉轻柔的滴答声）

这些听觉细节为读者创造了一个宁静的背景。

Touch：The softness of the grass beneath my feet（脚下草地的柔软）

the coolness of the pond water on my skin（皮肤上池塘水的凉爽）

这些描述让读者感受到公园的质地和温度，增强了沉浸式体验。

通过结合五种感官，这段文字创造了一个丰富而沉浸式的公园描述，让读者能够以多种感官的方式去感受。

（四）技巧归纳

首先，学生需要从五种感官及内心感受等角度去仔细观察，并思考所选地点的一些特点，以便在写作时进行生动细致的刻画。接下来是构思写作框架，学生需要注意文章如何开头、如何完成主体、如何收尾这三个方面。好的开头要引人入胜，能够激起读者的兴趣与读下去的渴望。比如，可以通过呈现所要介绍地点的一个特色鲜明的画面，或是其出人意料的某个方面，或是引用和该地点相关的名言和谚语，或是提出一个问题等手法，来抓住读者的注意力。主体部分要做好衔接，比如可以通过一些表示空间或顺序的逻辑词使读者能够跟上文章的描写思路。同时，要避免使用模糊、过于宽泛的措辞，而是生动地刻画细节并通过举例使描写更加具体、准确。结尾部分要收尾自然，通过高度浓缩或意味深远的语言给读者留下深刻的印象。

（五）迁移创新

使用“五感写作法”描写一个你游览过的地方。

（六）作品舞台

学生作品 1

Finally it was the National Day holiday! My parents and I went to Indonesia to see komodo dragons.

I saw two komodo dragons, which had big mouths, long tails and strong legs. They were very big, just like adults. One komodo dragon was drinking water, while the other was hiding under a staircase. I heard the guide. He said komodo dragons live in holes and baby komodo dragons can climb trees. I pretended to touch the komodo dragon when I was taking a photo. But I can't really touch it because it will bite me and it's poisonous and I will die.

At last we went back home and I was excited. I hope I would see komodo dragons again!

教师点评：

"I saw two komodo dragons, which had big mouths, long tails and strong legs." "They were very big, just like adults." "One komodo dragon was drinking water, while the other was hiding under a staircase."是视觉描写，"I heard the guide." "He said komodo dragons live in holes and baby komodo dragons can climb trees." 是听觉描写，故本篇习作主要利用的是视觉和听觉描写。

学生作品 2

During this summer vacation, my family went to the historic city of Rome.

Upon arrival, we were picked up at a very busy and noisy airport. Rome was not the same as America, for the buildings there were very old but very fancy. The first place we visited was the Colosseum. When I put my hands on the wall, I felt I could feel history! I listened as the tour guide told us the history of the Colosseum and how it was built by the ancient Romans. I enjoyed it very much, but my little brother thought it was boring. The smell of pizza made him hungry and he just wanted to go to a restaurant.

After the sightseeing, my father treated us to some ice cream, which tasted so sweet and delicious. We had a great day and I couldn't wait to see more of Rome!

教师点评：

本文很好地使用了"五感写作法"：a very busy and noisy airport 是视觉、听觉描写，the buildings there were very old but very fancy 是视觉描写，"When I put my hands on the wall, I felt I could feel history!"是触觉描写，The smell of pizza made him hungry 是嗅觉描写，which tasted so sweet and delicious 是味觉描写。

二、节日介绍法

（一）类别解析

介绍一个国家或地方，常常会介绍当地的传统节日。节日的介绍可以包括节日的起源、时间、庆祝活动、特色美食、盛装服饰、发展历史、意义等方面。

（二）精研文本

人教版新教材必修第三册第一单元中的 *Why Do We Celebrate Festivals*? 是一篇关于人们为何庆祝节日的文章，文中也列举了不少节日做例子。我们来梳理一下这篇文章都涵盖了节日的哪些方面。

节日的起源	They have a wide range of origins, such as the seasons of the year, religions, famous figures, and important events.
节日的时间	This important agricultural festival takes place after all the crops have been gathered in. In ancient Egypt, the harvest festival was celebrated during the springtime.
节日的庆祝活动	People decorate churches and town halls with flowers and fruit, and get together to celebrate over a meal. Families gather to admire the shining moon and enjoy delicious mooncakes.
节日的特色	It featured a parade and a great feast with music, dancing, and sports.
节日传统的变化与发展	Customs play a significant role in festivals, but sometimes they can change over time. With the development of modern society and the spread of new ideas, some traditions may fade away and others may be established.
节日的意义	Every festival has its different customs and unique charms. However, no matter how different they may seem, all over the world, the spirit of sharing joy, gratitude, love, or peace is common in all festivals. People celebrate to show that they are grateful for the year's supply of food. They reflect people's wishes, beliefs, faiths, and attitudes towards life. They are occasions that allow us to relax and enjoy life, and forget about our work for a little while. They help us understand where we come from, who we are, and what to appreciate.

从文中我们可以看出，介绍节日可以写节日的起源、节日的时间、节日的庆祝活动、节日的特色、节日传统的变化与发展、节日的意义等方面。此外，还可以根据具体的写作要求，如需要涵盖的写作要点、写作字数等，加以取舍，完成作文。

译林版新教材必修第三册第三单元 Extended Reading 部分的文章 *A Precious Family Dinner* 主要介绍的是中国的春节。下面我们也用表格的形式梳理一下文章内容。

节日的时间	the Chinese New Year's Eve
节日的食物	… the dinner table is already covered with white china plates and bowls, full of all sorts of dishes: chicken, duck, pork, fish and vegetables.
节日的装饰	Their home has been specially decorated for the joyous occasion. From the neat designs of the papercuttings on the windows, to the Spring Festival couplets on the door, and to the New Year paintings on the wall, everything represents joy, luck and happiness. Even the fish on the plate expresses a hope for *nian nian you yu*—*yu* means both "fish" and "plenty" in Chinese—"May you get more than you wish for every year."
节日的庆祝活动	The Luo family's journey back to their hometown was a long and tiring one just a few years ago. However, the high-speed train has made it much more convenient for them to go back home. The whole family are going to stay up late on the Chinese New Year's Eve. They gather around the television to watch the Spring Festival Gala, while eating snacks, chatting with each other and making dumplings that they will eat at the very start of the new year. In the warmth and comfort of the room, Luo Yan talks about his plan for the future. As midnight approaches, Luo Yan takes his parents, wife and son outside to set off firecrackers. The whole village is lit up with colorful fireworks.
节日的意义	All over the country, people are celebrating their good fortune, celebrating their family's togetherness, and celebrating their nation's strength.

因为春节是非常具有中国特色的节日，也是全球华人共同的传统节日，读者对其非常熟悉，所以作者把重点放在介绍春节的装饰和庆祝活动上。这篇文章也给学生写作春节主题的作文提供了非常标准的模板。

（三）课例展示

教材：外研版新教材必修第二册第二单元 Developing Ideas 板块的文本 *Time for a Change?*

文本分析：本板块中，两个读者针对报纸所提供的话题，分别写信发表了关于除夕团圆饭地点的不同看法。第一封信赞同在饭店吃饭，认为准备年夜饭很麻烦，需要很多时间和精力，而且不用做饭大家都无须劳碌，饭菜口味也更好。第二封信反对外出吃饭，认为这背离了悠久的传统，分离了一年之后全家人聚在一起准备年夜饭的过程远比食物本身更重要。两封信在陈述观点时引用了充分的论据，列举了除夕节日的传统和意义，以及节日和亲情的联系。

教学目标

1. 通过略读和详读，获取课文中不同人物的观点，梳理和概括理由；
2. 理解不同观点背后的原因和体现的价值观，增加对文化内涵的理解；
3. 能够对不同观点做出自己的评价和判断，提高批判性思维能力。

教学步骤

Activity 1：Lead-in

看教材 20 页上的图片，说一说春节的习俗。

参考答案：Pasting the character "fu" to the door and hang red lanterns

Playing waist drums　Letting off fireworks

Giving and receiving a red envelope/lucky money

继续追问：Can you think of other Chinese Spring Festival traditions?

参考答案：Watching the Spring Festival Gala on TV

Having a family reunion dinner on the New Year's Eve

Activity 2：Prediction

阅读标题及所配图片，预测：What might be changed?

参考答案：The ways of observing the Spring Festival might be changed.

Activity 3：Fast reading

让学生快速阅读 Social Insights 部分，完成以下问题及填空。

1) What might be changed?

2) What are people's opinions?

3) Where does the text probably come from?

4) Read for the main idea of each passage.

Passage 1 mainly tells us ________ enjoys ________ for the Spring Festival family dinner and he thinks it ________ loss of traditions.

Passage 2 mainly tells us __________ likes __________ for the Spring Festival family dinner and he thinks the process is even __________ than the dinner itself.

参考答案：

1) The ways of having Spring Festival family dinner might be changed.

2) Nowadays, some people choose to have the dinner in a restaurant, but not everyone is keen on the idea.

3) A newspaper.

4) Wang Peng, eating out, has nothing to do with, Liu Yonghui, eating at home, more important

Activity 4: Careful reading

仔细阅读两封读者来信，了解两位读者的观点。

Name	__________, software engineer
Opinion	Enjoy eating __________ on Spring Festival
Evidence	1. Preparations for dinner are ______________ and they spend too much ______________. 2. The occasion is more ______________ without all that tiring ______________ and ______________ taste better.
Conclusion	Eating out may change the ______________ of the tradition but the ______________ remains the same.

参考答案：Wang Peng, out, hard work, time and effort, enjoyable, cooking, the dishes, form, love

Name	__________, retired teacher
Opinion	Prefer to eat at __________
Evidence	The dinner on the eve of Spring Festival was not only for the __________ that we seldom got to eat, but for the opportunity to have our whole family __________.
Conclusion	The __________ is even more important than the dinner itself.

参考答案：Liu Yonghui, home, delicious food, gathered together, process

Activity 5: Post reading

Tell the difference between a fact and an opinion.

A fact is something that exists or has happened, for example, an object, event or experience. Facts are statements that can be proved by evidence.

An opinion can be a general or individual view, belief or impression. Opinions can sometimes be identified by the presence of words such as "feel" "believe" and "think".

让学生判断下列文中的句子是事实还是观点。

1. Eating out is a good choice and it has nothing to do with loss of traditions. ________
2. … what or where we eat on Spring Festival Eve really doesn't matter. ________
3. … it just won't feel like Spring Festival having the dinner out. ________
4. I'd get under my mother's feet in the kitchen, watching her make dumplings. ________
5. She'd put tokens in some dumplings… ________

参考答案:OOOFF

Activity 6: Discussion

提出问题,让学生讨论并发表观点。

Which of the two opinions do you agree with? Why?

Activity 7: Homework

给该报纸写一封信,阐述自己关于除夕团圆饭地点的观点。

(四)技巧归纳

描写节日首先要介绍节日起源。节日起源通常有宗教性节日、纪念历史重要人物或事件、庆祝丰收和庆祝季节等。然后介绍节日的时间,是公历还是农历?每年的哪一天?节日持续几天?接下来介绍节日的庆祝活动,这也是节日最热闹的部分。庆祝活动可谓多种多样,比如歌舞表演、游行活动、祝祷仪式、洒扫装饰、制作美食、祭祀祖先、竞技比赛等。节日的发展变化通常是指随着时间和人们生活方式的变化,庆祝节日的方式和传统也发生了改变。最后总结节日的意义:家人团聚、凝聚亲情、分享喜悦、追忆祖先、致敬伟人、铭记历史、弘扬文化、寄托希望、表达祝福、感悟人生等。常用的表达如下:

1)节日的起源

originate in 起源于……	have its origins in… 起源于……
date back to… 最早追溯到……	have a religious origin 起源于宗教
in memory of… 为了纪念……	in honor of… 向……致敬

2)节日的时间

take place on… 在……举行	is celebrated on… 在……庆祝

fall on the calendar… 时间是……

3)节日的庆祝活动

decorate… with… 用……装饰…… celebrate by… 用……庆祝

a feast for the eyes 视觉盛宴 celebrate over a meal 吃大餐庆祝

admire the moon 赏月 take part in games 参加游戏

4)节日的特色

It features… 以……为特色

5)节日传统的变化发展

remain the same 维持不变

change a little/a lot over time 随着时间变化很小/很大

traditions fade away and others were established 旧传统消失,新习俗建立

6)节日的意义

the spirit of sharing joy, gratitude, love or peace 分享快乐、感恩、爱或和平的精神

be thankful/grateful to sb for sth 因为某事感激某人

reflect people's wishes, beliefs, faiths and attitudes towards life

反映人们的愿望、信念、信仰和对生活的态度

allow us to relax and enjoy life, and forget about our work

让我们放松,享受生活,忘记工作

help us understand where we came from, who we are, and what to appreciate

帮助我们了解我们来自哪里,我们是谁,以及应该感激什么

(五)迁移创新

假设你是学校英语俱乐部的成员,该俱乐部将举办主题为"How Did You Spend This Spring Festival?"的交流活动。请你用英语写一篇发言稿,届时与大家分享。内容包括:

1. 你是怎样过这个春节的;
2. 你的感受或收获是什么。

注意:

1. 词数 100 左右,开头和结尾已给出,不计入总词数;
2. 可以适当增加细节,以使行文连贯。

Hello, everyone! I'm honored to share with you how I spent this Spring Festival.

____

____

____

____

Thanks for listening!

（六）作品舞台

学生作品 1

Hello, everyone! I'm honored to share with you how I spent this Spring Festival.

During the Spring Festival, I got up early as I couldn't wait to visit my grandparents with presents elaborately prepared. With joy they gave me lucky money, which carried their best wishes. Under their instruction, I tried to make dumplings. It's a tradition that family members get together and enjoy a delicious meal, which is believed to bring good luck. This year, I was fortunate enough to accompany them and appreciate firework performances.

I consider the Spring Festival as an auspicious festival to connect us with our family members. With family get-togethers, we enjoy pleasure, relieve stress and have hope for the new year. I really treasure the time spent with my relatives.

If you're available, I'm also interested to know what you did in the Spring Festival.

Thanks for listening!

教师点评：

本篇书面表达的题目是:你是怎样过这个春节的。学生作品用了 elaborately、auspicious 等词汇和语块 couldn't wait to,也使用了两个 which 引导的定语从句,整体比较流畅。

学生作品 2

Hello, everyone! I'm honored to share with you how I spent this Spring Festival.

First and foremost, the Spring Festival being the essence of the Chinese culture, we extended a warm welcome to it. Apart from cleaning to wash away bad fortune, sharing dumplings and seniors' giving lucky money were a must. Subsequently, traveling was my second-to-none choice. The short stay in Shenzhen—a city blessed with radiant sunshine and dazzling beaches, made me exceedingly elated. Simultaneously, so relentless was my pursuit for a top university that I put in much enthusiasm and endeavor to improve my academic performances, hoping my sweat pays off this summer.

As for my harvest, the Spring Festival is a golden chance to eradicate unpleasant memories, turn to a new page and say hi to the new year ebulliently. Let's create a worth-living 2023!

Thanks for listening!

教师点评：

这篇文章使用了很多高级词汇,如 essence、subsequently、second-to-none、radiant、dazzling、exceedingly、elated、simultaneously、relentless、enthusiasm、eradicate、ebulliently 等,关联词的使用也使得文章更有条理性(First and foremost, Apart from, Subsequently, Simultaneously),是一篇高分佳作。

三、地理位置，气候环境

（一）类别解析

介绍一个国家、城市或地方，一般会介绍它的所在位置及地理方面的特点，比如海拔、面积、河流、湖泊、山脉、地形等，以及其气候环境和天气特征。

（二）精研文本

人教版新教材必修第一册第二单元以一段小短文配上秘鲁的地图，简要介绍了秘鲁这个国家的地理位置：

Peru is a country on the Pacific coast of South America with three main areas: narrow, dry, flat land running along the coast, the Andes Mountains and the Amazon rainforest.

人教版旧教材必修第三册第五单元的阅读板块介绍了两位青少年乘坐火车横穿加拿大的旅行经历，文中也对加拿大的地理和气候进行了简洁的描写：

... but they forget the fact that Canada is 5,500 kilometers from coast to coast... People say it is Canada's most beautiful city, surrounded by mountains and the Pacific Ocean... The coast north of Vancouver has some of the oldest and most beautiful forests in the world. It is so wet there that the trees are extremely tall, some measuring over 90 meters.

译林版新教材必修第三册第一单元 Reading 板块的课文 *The Amazon Rainforest: a Natural Treasure* 介绍了亚马逊雨林的地理位置及面积、长度等特点：

The Amazon rainforest crosses into eight countries, including Brazil and Peru, and one overseas region of France, all on the South American continent. With an area of around 6 million square kilometers, the Amazon rainforest is more than half the size of China. The Amazon River, from which the rainforest gets its name, is close to 6,400 kilometers in length—roughly 100 kilometers longer than the Yangtze River.

（三）课例展示

教材：译林版新教材选择性必修第三册第一单元 Reading 板块的文本 *Canada—a Land of Diversity*

文本分析：本单元主要围绕旅游与文化差异展开。教材内容涵盖了旅游地点、文化习俗以及不同国家的特色景点等。本篇文章主要介绍了加拿大是一个充满多样性的国家，并通过中间三个段落分别讲述了其地理、民族及文化的多样性。

教学目标

1. 学生能够了解并描述不同国家和城市的旅游景点、文化习俗以及相关信息；

2. 通过阅读，学生能够理解文章中提供的信息并提取相关细节，能够用英语进行简单的口头表达；

3. 培养学生对不同国家和文化的了解与尊重，培养学生的跨文化交流和合作意识。

教学步骤

Activity 1：Lead-in

教师播放一段视频，让学生思考"Which country is it about?"由视频中的加拿大的典型元素，学生可以知道视频是在推介加拿大的旅游。

Activity 2：A quiz

通过小测验的形式对加拿大的背景知识进行补充，为下面的阅读环节做铺垫。

1）Canada is the ________ largest country in the world.

A. first　　B. second　　C. third

2）Which date is Canada Day（加拿大国庆日）？

A. February 1th.　　B. July 1th.　　C. July 4th.

3）Which city is Canada's capital?

A. Montreal.　　B. Ottawa.　　C. Vancouver.

4）Which of the following are Canada's national symbols?

A. Beaver.　　B. Maple trees.　　C. Ice hockey（冰上曲棍球）.

参考答案：1）B　2）B　3）B　4）ABC

Activity 3：Skimming

学生略读课文，概括段落大意，然后根据段落大意划分文章结构。

参考答案：

Paragraph 1：Canada is a broad country with diverse ethnic groups.

Paragraph 2：Canada is geographically diverse.

Paragraph 3：Canada is ethnically diverse.

Paragraph 4：Canada is culturally diverse.

Paragraph 5：Canada is a unique place to live in and visit.

可以把文章分为三个部分，第一段和第五段分别是第一部分和第三部分，第二段到第四段为第二部分，按照 Introduction—Body—Conclusion 的顺序行文。

Activity 4: Careful reading

教师首先呈现 True or False 问题,接着让学生仔细阅读课文。

( ) 1) The grand Rocky Mountains rise to the west of the Pacific coast.

( ) 2) Canada's many rural areas and urban centers can reflect the diversity of Canada's cultures.

( ) 3) You feel the subcultures in languages, cuisine, architecture, art and music in Canada.

( ) 4) You can dance to fiddle tunes and enjoy the cultures and traditions of Chinese settlers on Cape Breton Island.

( ) 5) Its geographical wonders, ethnic groups and their cultures make Canada a unique place to live in and visit.

参考答案:FFTFT

教师再通过选择题引导学生对文本进行深度挖掘。

1) Which of the following descriptions of Canada is TRUE according to Paragraph 2?

A. Canada is made up of ten provinces and four territories.

B. The mighty Niagara Falls are a unique scenic spot in Canada.

C. The grand Rocky Mountains lie along the Pacific coastline.

D. The public are forbidden to visit the national parks such as Banff and Jasper National Parks.

2) Who are called the minority groups in Canada?

A. The English. B. The Scottish.

C. The French. D. Residents from Singapore and the Pacific Islands.

3) What do you most probably do if you are in Montreal?

A. Sampling the food with a typical French flavor.

B. Participating in the celebrations of the Chinese New Year.

C. Taking tea in the Dr Sun Yat-Sen Classical Chinese Garden.

D. Seeing the original buildings in the English style of architecture.

4) Which of the following is NOT a factor that makes Canada a unique place to live in and visit?

A. Its geographical wonders. B. Its ethnic groups.

C. Its delicious food. D. Its diverse cultures.

参考答案:BDAC

Activity 5: Consolidation

学生完成语篇填空,对课文进行巩固。

Canada is not only a broad and beautiful country but also one of the most 1) ________ (ethnic) diverse nations in the world with distinct cultures.

In the ten provinces and three 2) ________ (territory) which make up Canada, there is great diversity in geography. Besides, Canada's many rural areas and urban centers reflect the diversity of its residents. 3) ________ is thought that some of Canada's earliest settlers 4) ________ (cross) the Bering Strait by means of a land bridge from Siberia thousands of years ago. Today, Canada reflects a vast 5) ________ (combine) of ethnic backgrounds. One out of five people in Canada's population is foreign-born. This ethnic variety, in turn, brings about cultural diversity. As you are exposed 6) ________ diverse cultures, you may feel transported through time and space. 7) ________ (give) these cultural differences, it comes as no surprise 8) ________ Canada has been celebrating Multiculturalism Day since 2002.

From the towering mountain peaks to the depths of the forests to the urban centers, Canada's geographical wonders, ethnic groups and their cultures make it a unique place 9) ________ (live) in and visit. Indeed, it has been consistently ranked by the United Nations as one of the 10) ________ (good) countries to live in, and visitors are always welcome!

参考答案：1) ethnically　2) territories　3) It　4) crossed　5) combination
6) to　7) Given　8) that　9) to live　10) best

Activity 6：Discussion

本环节是学习课文之后的迁移创新环节，旨在让学生学以致用，介绍中国的多样性。

If we are to demonstrate China's diversity to foreigners, what aspects should we start from?

参考答案：

Geography	land, forests, mountains, lakes/rivers, wildlife...
People	ethnic diversity, residents from rural/urban areas...
Culture	languages, cuisine, architecture, art, music...

Activity 7：Homework

作业1：写一篇短文，介绍中国的地理多样性。

作业2：口头演讲，介绍中国的地理多样性。

学生作业展示：

China is a vast land stretching from the Himalayas to the East China Sea, dotted with vibrant forests, clear lakes and towering mountains. To the west rise major mountain ranges, most notably the Himalayas. Southern China is dominated by hills and low mountain ranges, while the central-east hosts deltas of China's two major rivers, the Yellow River and the Yangtze River.

China is like a blooming flower, unveiling its uniqueness and beauty to those who wait to explore it. Welcome to China!

（四）技巧归纳

介绍地理位置和气候环境的常用表达如下：

位置：

Located in Dengfeng City of Henan Province, Songshan Mountain is called the Central Mountain of the Five Sacred Mountains.

位于河南省登封市的嵩山被称为“五岳”中的“中岳”。

Qinghai Lake National Nature Reserve is located in the northeast of the Qinghai-Tibet Plateau at the southern foot of the Qilian Mountains in Qinghai Province.

青海湖国家级自然保护区位于青藏高原东北部，青海省祁连山南麓。

海拔/高度：

It is... meters tall/high./It is... meters in height.　它高……米。

At this altitude you often get strong winds.　这一纬度地区经常有大风。

面积：

It covers an area of... square meters.　它占地……平方米。

The farm is about 50 square kilometers in area.

这个农场的面积约为 50 平方公里。

河流：

A river forms the boundary between the two countries.　一条河成了两国的分界线。

The course of this river used to be quite irregular.　这条河的水道原来很不规则。

The river pours itself into the sea.　这条河流入大海。

Rivers and torrents carried great loads of sediment out to sea.

河流挟着大量沉积物奔流入海。

湖泊：

At the center of the lake, there is a pavilion.　湖心有一座亭子。

The lake has a depth of 300 feet in the middle.　湖中心水深为三百英尺。

The West Lake is as beautiful as a painting.　西湖风景如画。

山脉：

A gentle breeze from the Blue Ridge Mountains carried the scent of honeysuckle.

从蓝岭山脉吹过来的和风带来了忍冬花的芬芳。

Through these mountains a foot-track traverses the passes and the virgin jungle.

这片山脉中有一条羊肠小道,穿过各个隘口和原始丛林。

He got up, gazing down at the town, at the plain all green with crops and the mountains glamorous in sinking sunlight.

他站起来,俯视着这座城镇,看着麦田青青的平原和在夕阳下闪闪发光的群山。

天气:

It was a beast of a day, bleak, cold, and rainy. 这天天气恶劣,冷风凄雨。

The weather became finer and more settled. 天气逐渐转晴并稳定下来。

The wind and rain slowly change the shapes of the mountains, creating strange forms that resemble tower, peaks, rounded hills and saw teeth.

风雨渐渐改变山脉的形状,形成奇怪的形状,仿佛是楼塔、尖顶、圆形山丘或是锯齿。

(五)迁移创新

翻译下面的语段:

青海湖在不同的季节有着不同的风景。春天,周围的山脉和湿地呈现出清新的绿色,散布着五颜六色的花朵和白雪。你可以住在青海湖边,见证冰川融化,迎接成千上万远道而来的客人——候鸟(migratory birds)。夏秋两季,湖面披上了金色的衣裳,数万公顷的油菜花(rape flowers)从青海湖岸蔓延开来。冬天,冰雪覆盖湖面,湖面变得安静。这是一个让你放慢脚步,沉浸在寒冷的世界中,欣赏宁静的高原(plateau)风光的好时机。

(六)作品舞台

学生作品 1

The scenery differs a lot in different seasons in Qinghai Lake. In spring, the nearby mountains and wetlands are crisp green, strewn with colorful flowers and white snow. You can live on the edge of Qinghai Lake, eyewitness the glaciers' melting, and greet thousands of visitors from faraway places—migratory birds. In summer and autumn, the lake covered with golden clothes, tens of thousands of hectares of rape flowers spread out from the shores of Qinghai Lake. In winter, ice and snow cover the lake, causing it to be quite quiet. This is a golden time for you to slow down, indulge yourself in the cold world and enjoy the tranquil plateau scenery.

教师点评:

译文基本遵循了原文的行文顺序与结构安排,词块、语块的使用富于变化,体现了较强的语言综合运用能力,如 differ in(在某方面有所不同)、strewn with(撒满……的;布满……的)、独立主格结构(the lake covered with golden clothes)、分词作结果状语(causing it to be quite quiet)等。

学生作品2

Qinghai Lake has very different sceneries in different seasons.

In spring, the surrounding mountains and wetlands take on a fresh green look with scattered colorful flowers and white snow. You can stay beside Qinghai Lake, witness the melting ice, and welcome thousands of guests from afar—migratory birds.

In summer and autumn, the lake is decorated with golden clothing, as tens of thousands of hectares of rape flowers spread out from Qinghai Lake's shores.

In winter, snow and ice cover the surface of the lake, and the lake becomes quiet. It's a good time for you to go and slow your pace, immerse yourself in the cold world, and enjoy the quiet plateau scenery.

教师点评：

译文在结构上与原文并不相同。原文是一个段落,译文则分为了四个小段落。其中,第一段是总起句,第二、三、四段分别介绍春天、夏秋、冬天的青海湖。本文中词块、语块的使用也很精彩,如 take on a... look(呈现出……)、be decorated with(装饰着……)、immerse oneself in...(沉浸在……中)等。

四、人文历史，城市足迹

（一）类别解析

介绍一个国家、城市或地方,通常也会介绍它的发展历史,包括城市变迁、人口迁徙、历史地位、重大事件、重要历史人物等。

（二）精研文本

人教版新教材必修第一册第二单元中的一篇小短文简要介绍了秘鲁这个国家的部分历史：

In the 1400s and 1500s, Peru was the center of the powerful ancient Inca Empire. ... Spain took control of Peru in the 16th century and ruled until 1821.

译林版新教材选择性必修第三册第一单元 Reading 板块的文章 *Canada—a Land of Diversity* 介绍了加拿大的历史：

Apart from its geographical diversity, Canada's many rural areas and urban centers reflect the diversity of its residents. Some of Canada's earliest settlers, who are thought to be ancestors of the indigenous peoples, crossed the Bering Strait by means of a land bridge from a place now known as

Siberia. They settled on this vast land thousands of years ago. The first Europeans also started to settle in some of the eastern provinces centuries ago. Today, Canada reflects a vast combination of ethnic backgrounds. About one out of five people in Canada's population is foreign-born. The major ethnic groups, for example, include the English, Scottish and French, while the minority groups include residents from Singapore and the Pacific Islands.

人教版旧教材选修第八册第一单元阅读板块中的 *California* 是一篇介绍美国加州移民历史的文章，从加州土著到第一批西班牙外来殖民者的到来，再到后来的俄国定居者，以及西部淘金热吸引来的来自世界其他地方的移民，还有近几十年间来自亚洲的大批移民，形成了加州多种族聚居、多元文化并存的面貌：

... the majority were religious men, whose ministry was to teach the Catholic religion to the natives. In 1821, the people of Mexico gained their independence from Spain. California then became part of Mexico. In 1846 the United States declared war on Mexico... In the early 1800s, Russian hunters, who had originally gone to Alaska, began settling in California. ... Today, Chinese-Americans live in all parts of California, although a large percentage have chosen to stay in the "Chinatowns" of Los Angeles and San Francisco. ... People from Africa have been living in California since the 1800s, ... However, even more arrived between 1942 and 1945 to work in the ship and aircraft industries. ... In more recent decades, California has become home to more people from Asia, including Koreans, Cambodians, Vietnamese and Laotians... People from different parts of the world, attracted by the climate and lifestyle, still immigrate to California.

（三）课例展示

教材：人教版新教材必修第二册第四单元 Reading and Thinking 板块的文本 *What's in a Name?*

文本分析：本单元以历史和传统为主题，涉及多个国家的悠久历史和文化传统等内容。在悠久的历史文化长河中，这些国家孕育了一些特有的文化传统和风俗习惯。了解这些历史和传统，对学生理解英语语言、世界重要文明的历史文化内涵及其蕴含的思维方式，都具有重要的意义。文本是一篇说明文，介绍了英国历史的简要发展进程。学生通过阅读课文了解英国的地理、社会及文化概况，并深入思考历史与社会文化之间的关系。文本包含五个段落。第一段通过设问引出话题：为何用不同的名字指称英国？第二段写英国的建国史；第三段写四个国家合作和独立行事的领域；第四段写英国历史上的四个种族以及各种族对英国文化的影响；第五段是给旅英人士的建议。这篇文章在全书乃至整个高中阶段都有重要的作用。英国历史悠久，文化繁荣，具有一定的国际影响力，了解其历史和文化，是每个英语学习者的必修课。文中出现了多个高考核心词汇和语法结构。在历年的高考题中，多次出现以英国为背景的阅读和写作题型。这篇文章也为同一单元其他板块的学习做了铺垫。文中出现了很多关于英国历史的介绍，比如：

In the 16th century, the nearby country of Wales was joined to the Kingdom of England. Later, in the 18th century, the country Scotland was joined to create the Kingdom of Great Britain. In the19th century, the Kingdom of Ireland was added to create the United Kingdom of Great Britain and Ireland. Finally, in the 20th century, the southern part of Ireland broke away from the UK, which resulted in the full name we have today: the United Kingdom of Great Britain and Northern Ireland. ...The United Kingdom has a long and interesting history to explore, which can help you understand much more about the country and its traditions. ... four different groups of people who took over at different times throughout history. ... Some of their great achievements included building towns and roads. ... They introduced the beginnings of the English language. ... They conquered England after the well-known Battle of Hastings in the 11th century. They had castles built all around England, and made changes to the legal system. ... is an ancient port city that has a history dating all the way back to Roman times.

教学目标

1. 了解英国的地理特征、名字由来、历史重大事件和对语言、文化产生的影响；
2. 训练阅读技巧，寻找段落大意；
3. 学会介绍历史和文化的词块、语块，介绍当地文化给外国友人。

教学步骤

Activity 1: Free talk

教师呈现几幅不同的英国地图，提问：

1) What differences do they have?

2) What do the symbols on the first map represent?

3) What does the UK consist of?

学生通过读图可以发现，几幅图分别是行政区划图(administrative zoning map)、地形图(topographic map)、交通图(traffic map)、气象图(weather map)和资源图(resource map)，并在此基础上对英国有了一个整体的感知与认识，为文章的学习打下基础。从行政区划图可以看到，不同的国家使用了不同的颜色，学生由此可知大不列颠及北爱尔兰联合王国(The United Kingdom of Great Britain and Northern Ireland)，简称“英国”，由四个部分组成：英格兰、威尔士、苏格兰和北爱尔兰，首都为伦敦。

Activity 2: Prediction

学生通过阅读文章标题对文章内容进行预测，形成阅读期待。

Activity 3：Reading

Step 1. Skimming

首先要求学生快速略读，即不追求句子的细节含义，只了解句子和段落想表达的内容，弄清楚段落的主旨大意，然后让学生根据段落大意划分文章结构。为降低难度，可以给学生一个表格来帮助他们获取段落大意。

Paragraphs	Main Ideas
Para. 1	Getting to know British ______ helps you solve the puzzle of different ______ of the country
Para. 2	How we get the ______ name of the country
Para. 3	The ______ and ______ between four countries within the UK
Para. 4	The history of the UK helps you learn more about the ______ and ______
Para. 5	Learning the country's history makes your visit more ______

参考答案：history，names，full，similarities，differences，country，traditions，enjoyable

教师提示学生：主题句经常出现在段首或段末。这样学生就可以快速找到主题句，继而把文章分为三个部分：第一到第三段是第一部分（The history of the UK helps us understand why the UK has different names）；第四段和第五段分别是第二和第三部分。根据三个部分的大意可以总结出全文大意：Advantages of studying British history。

Step 2. Detailed reading

1. 提出问题："How does the author introduces the topic of this passage?"让学生读第一段。

参考答案：Puzzle→History 即 Question→Solution。

2. 让学生读第二、三两段，按照时间线梳理信息。

16th century：　　　　+　　　　=

18th century：　　　　+　　　　=

19th century：　　　　+　　　　=

20th century：　　　　−　　　　=

参考答案：

- 16th century：Wales + England= England
- 18th century：Scotland + England = Great Britain
- 19th century：Ireland + Great Britain = The United Kingdom of Great Britain and Ireland
- 20th century：The United Kingdom of Great Britain and Ireland − Republic of Ireland = The United Kingdom of Great Britain and Northern Ireland

根据此时间线可知,本文是按照时间的顺序展开的。学生在写作类似的文章时也可以按照时间的顺序来写。

3. 提出问题:"What did the new arrivals do in the 1st, 5th, 8th and 11th century?"让学生读第四段。

参考答案：

In the 1st century：Romans—towns & roads

In the 5th century：Anglo-Saxons—houses & language

In the 8th century：Vikings—vocabulary & names

In the 11th century：Normans—French words & legal systems & castles

Activity 4：In-depth reading

提出两个问题：

1）Who do you think are the intended readers of this passage?

2）Why is studying the history of one country of great significance?

参考答案：

1）People who would like to visit the UK or want to know its history.

2）Because it can help us understand a country's past and its present. Besides, we can use what we learn to know what we will do and what we should do in the future.

Marcus Garvey 的名言"A people without the knowledge of their past history, origin and culture is like a tree without roots."或许能给我们提供答案:知史鉴今。

Activity 5：Group discussion

1）If you were to give foreigners some suggestions on visiting China, which period of China's long history would you advise them to study before their visit?

2）Which city do you think is a great place for the foreigners to start in China?

Activity 6: Homework

Your foreign friend Jim is planning to visit China this year and is asking you for some suggestions. Please write him an email. You are expected to talk about the advantages of studying Chinese history and recommend a great place to start to visit in China.

参考范文:

Dear Jim,

Delighted to hear that you intend to visit China, I'm writing to share with you some suggestions.

Knowing a little Chinese history will be helpful when you visit China. Not only can it help you understand a lot about our country and our traditions, but it can also make your visit much more enjoyable.

If you visit China, I recommend that Xi'an should be a great place to start. It's an ancient city with a centuries-old history. There are countless historic sites for you to explore, and lots of museums with ancient items from all over China. If you keep your eyes open, you will be surprised to find that you can see both its past and its present.

Looking forward to your arrival.

Yours,

Li Hua

(四)技巧归纳

一个国家、城市或地方的历史发展历程通常比较复杂,需要较多的笔墨才能写得清楚,因此我们可以把重点放到历史地位、重大事件、重要历史人物等几个方面。下面几个句子仅供参考:

About half of South Korea's population lives in the Seoul National Capital Area, and one quarter in Seoul itself, making it the country's political, cultural and economic center.

韩国大约一半的人口居住在首尔国家首都区,四分之一的人口居住在首尔本身,使其成为韩国的政治、文化和经济中心。

The rapid economic, social and technological development of Seoul has played a key role in South Korea's development and has been referred to as the "Miracle on the Han River".

首尔经济、社会和科技的快速发展对韩国的发展起到了关键作用,被称为"汉江上的奇迹"。

Seoul hosts more than three million registered vehicles and widespread traffic congestion is common. In recent years, the metropolitan government has undertaken extensive cleaning-up of the city's air and water pollution.

首尔有逾三百万辆注册车辆,交通堵塞是常见现象。近年来,这个大都市政府对城市的空气和水污染进行了大规模的清理。

(五)迁移创新

用英语写一个段落,介绍一下你的家乡,词数80左右。

(六)作品舞台

学生作品1

My hometown is a new and developing city, and was built at the beginning of 1970s. The infrastructure for water, gas, electricity and other energy is complete and sufficient. From here, one can travel to any place by land, by sea or by air. And there is a highway leading to the capital—Beijing. That is to say, if you want to visit well-known places of interest in the capital, it will be very convenient to set off from my hometown.

教师点评:

本文虽然比较简单,但一些词汇的使用还是很高级的,如 infrastructure(基础设施)、sufficient(充足的)、set off(出发;动身)等,还使用了现在分词作后置定语(leading to the capital—Beijing)和插入语(That is to say)。

学生作品2

Everyone has his own favorite place buried deeply in heart. When it comes to my favorite place, my beloved hometown must surely be the first option rushing into my mind.

Embraced by Mount Song, my hometown enjoyed a clear blue sky and pure air most of the time. Every morning when I got up and opened the window, the sleepy mind would be greeted by the primitive chilly air produced by the trees and would be woken up immediately without any unwillingness.

After breakfast, my father and I would usually go out for a morning walk along the narrow paths lined with tall phoenix trees whose dense leaves avoided the strong vitalight shot from the sun and created interesting fragmental golden light spots on the roads. The extcited sparrows played heartfreely, so did I. Taking my father's hand, I loved to stand by the river bank across from our little bungallow, losing myself in admiring the happy water flowing down the stone bridge, entranced as the soft breeze swept over my cheeks.

After a long "exhausting" day "studying" in kindergarten, it came my long-awaited moment when my mother picked me up and bought me a fluffy piece of bread tipped with hot honey. On our way home, I would share my newly-learnt nursery rhymes with my mother, which would invariably win great praise.

教师点评:

本篇习作使用高级结构较多,分词及分词短语作定语(buried deeply in heart、rushing into my mind、produced by the trees、lined with tall phoenix trees、flowing down the stone bridge、"exhausting"、"studying" in kindergarten、long-awaited、tipped with hot honey、newly-learnt)和分词短语作状语(Embraced by Mount Song, Taking my father's hand, losing myself in...)比比皆是,可见作者语言基本功过硬,综合语言运用能力较强。

第三节　叙述事件

一、确定时间线,叙述有条理

(一)类别解析

记叙文通常会按事件发生的先后顺序对事件展开叙述,因为这样才能避免混乱,使文章显得有条理。常用的时间顺序有正序法、倒叙法和插叙法,其中以正序法最为常见。

(二)精研文本

人教版新教材必修第一册第四单元 Reading and Thinking 板块的 *The Night the Earth Didn't Sleep* 一文讲述的是 1976 年唐山大地震的情形。文章详细描述了地震发生之前的各种征兆、地震发生时各种可怕的景象、地震造成的破坏、地震之后如何积极开展救援活动和唐山人民在灾后重建家园的情况。作者在叙述唐山大地震的发生过程时使用了正序法,即按照时间顺序记述了唐山大地震的整个经过。作者运用了大量和时间相关的表达,按照"震前—震中—震后"的时间线,使整个故事犹如电影播放一般历历在目,叙述清晰而有条理。我们来看一下文章中用来叙述时间的表达都有哪些。

At about 3:00 **a.m.**, **on** 28 **July** 1976, bright lights were seen in the sky outside the city of Tangshan... **At** 3:42 **a.m.**, everything began to shake... **In less than one minute**, a large city lay in ruins... Sand **now** filled the wells instead of water. People were in shock—**and then**, **later that afternoon**, another big quake shook Tangshan again... **Soon after the quakes**, the army sent 150,000 soldiers to Tangshan to dig out those who were trapped…

新剑桥第三册第十一单元 Read and Listen 板块的 *A Service of Love* 是一篇改编自欧·亨利小说的节选文章，讲述了两个热爱艺术的年轻人在追求艺术的道路上相互扶持，为了成就彼此而做出自我牺牲的爱情故事。作者在讲述故事时使用了正序法，按照时间发展的顺序来展现两位主人公一路携手走来发生的故事。文章中和时间有关的表达很多：

But **soon**, the money began to run out and they couldn't afford lessons anymore. **Then one day** Delia came home and told Joe that she had met a man… **A few days later**, Joe came home and proudly took $200 from his pocket… So the two of them were happy **for a while**… **Then, one day**, Joe came home and saw that Delia's hand was wrapped in bandage.

故事中这些关于时间的表达使情节的发展显得非常清晰，两个艺术青年的生活点滴跃然纸上。

新剑桥第四册第七单元中有一篇介绍昂山素季的人物评论，作者在讲述昂山素季一生的经历时使用的也是正序法。从她的童年生活到求学经历，再到后来走上政治道路，在斗争中被政敌软禁 20 年后又重获自由，作者使用了大量和时间有关的表达：

When she was two years old, her father, who was expected to become prime minister of independent Burma, was assassinated. She went to school in Burma **until** 1960, **when** her mother became ambassador to India. **After** studying in India, she attended the University of Oxford… She had two children and lived a rather quiet life **until** 1988, **when** she returned to Myanmar to look after her mother who was very ill. **When** Aung San Suu Kyi arrived in her country, people were protesting against the rule of the military government… She **began** a non-violent struggle for democracy and human rights… Aung San Suu Kyi was placed under house arrest **from July** 1989… **Since** 1989, she has spent most of her time under house arrest, but **during this period** she has also been freed on several occasions. She was **finally** freed again from house arrest **on** 13 **November** 2010.

作者使用的这些关于时间的表达，使得昂山素季的人生故事像画卷一般在读者面前慢慢展开。

（三）课例展示

教材：北师大版新教材必修第二册第五单元的文本 *Race to the Pole*

文本分析：本单元属于"人与自然"主题语境，选用了不同体裁的文本，让学生从不同角度了解大自然并思考人与自然的关系。本单元讲述了海上漩涡奇遇、紧急救援、南极探险等人类与自然极端挑战展开拼搏的壮丽历程，帮助学生更好地认识人类与大自然的关系，培养学生敬畏自然、与自然和谐共存的意识。文本 *Race to the Pole* 的主题为“极地探险”，主要讲述了 20 世纪初来自英国的 Scott 和来自挪威的 Amundsen 这两位探险家的南极探险竞赛。文章按照“赛前准备—比赛过程—比赛结果”的顺序描述了两支队伍南极之旅的过程，并通过引用 Scott 的日记原文突出了 Scott 队伍在回程中所遇到的生死危机及队员们的情绪变化等史实。Scott 是本次南极竞赛失败的一方，但是作者用了大量篇幅描述他的探险过程，而对于获胜方 Amundsen 的描述则大多一笔带过。很明显，作者在文中把 Captain Scott 塑造为一个英雄的形象，通过带领学生在“极地探险”主题语境中梳理信息，了解 Scott 带领队伍进行南极探险的过程，感悟他所代表的敢为人先、勇于挑战极限、勇于探索、执着坚定、为人类福祉奋斗的英雄主义精神，引发学生对人生、个人命运以及人与自然的关系的思考。在研读文章标题 *Race to the Pole* 时，引导学生从理解 race 的表面意义（南极竞赛）到理解其深层含义（生与死、人与自然的竞赛）。在读后，通过讨论启发学生逐步认识到极地探险的危险性、未知性，从而敬畏大自然，能有“凡事皆要做好万全的准备”“不要仅凭借自己的努力或一腔热情”“在绝望场景下更要乐观积极”等态度。

文本在叙述两支队伍进行南极之旅比赛的过程时，按照时间顺序使用了正序法。

On 1 **June**, 1910, Captain Robert Falcon Scott left London to begin his journey to Antarctica. **While** he was on the way to Antarctica, he received a message… **Then** the race to the South Pole began! **During the polar summer of** 1910—1911, both teams organized food bases in preparation for their journeys the next year. **Then** came the total darkness of the polar winter… Amundsen was the first to leave **on** 8 **September**, 1911… Scott left **on** 1 **November** and **soon** had problems. **First**, his two sledges broke down and **then** the horses began to have serious difficulties with the snow and the cold. **After a while**, Scott and his men had to push the sledges themselves. Amundsen reached the Pole **on** 14 **December**, 1911 and put a Norwegian flag there. **Then** he prepared for the return journey. Amundsen and his team arrived safely back to their starting base **on** 25 **January**, 1912… Scott **finally** arrived at the Pole with four team members **on** 17 **January**, 1912… **Then** disaster came. Edgar Evans had a terrible disease and died… **The next to go** was Captain Oates, … **But then** a terrible storm started and they could not leave their tent…

文中使用了大量有关时间点和先后顺序的表达。

教学目标)))

1. 获取语篇大意及 Scott 和 Amundsen 南极探险之旅的过程等具体信息，梳理文章结构；
2. 感悟和阐释 Scott 的英雄主义特征；
3. 评价 Scott 的历史贡献，探索人与自然的关系。

教学步骤

Activity 1：Lead-in

教师呈现南极图片，提问：Do you know anything about it？随后呈现更多南极图片并让学生根据图片猜测南极的概况。随后，教师追问学生，面对南极困难的环境，是否愿意前往南极，如果遇到问题时会如何处理，如何看待坚持前往南极探险的人。学生思考并回答问题。

由于学生对南极大陆的认识不多，且这段探险的历史鲜为人知，学生在理解主人公的探险历程和心理变化方面可能会存在困难。因此，本活动通过介绍南极的概况，帮助学生了解南极的恶劣环境，使学生意识到南极探险之旅的危险和困难重重，让他们明白能够进行南极探险的人必定是坚定、勇敢的人，从而为随后阅读活动的开展做好铺垫。

Activity 2：Fast reading

1. 先呈现出 account 文体的定义，提醒学生在进行这一文体的阅读时应注意时间、地点、过程及作者的态度。

2. 依据 account 的文体特征，学生进行快速阅读——梳理本次竞赛发生的时间、地点，并初步理解文本标题的表面含义。

3. 细读文本，将教材上的练习 3 改编为“完成表格信息”的任务，把文本分成三部分：preparation、process、results，从而梳理出两支队伍的前期准备、出发时间、到达时间、旅途中发生的事情等。学生依据表格完成细节理解。在活动中，以图片和文字的形式向学生提供队伍所用工具、交通方式等相关背景史实，帮助学生从多方面了解两支队伍在准备过程中的异同，以更好地评价人物。

本活动主要是让学生准确理解文本内容，厘清文章线索。表格对照式的呈现方式有利于增强探险过程的画面感，突出英雄人物的悲壮色彩。同时，引导学生理解文本标题的含义，为后面对标题的深层理解做铺垫。将文本分成 preparation、process、results 三个部分能更好地突出事件中的因果关系。

Activity 3：Careful reading

1. 引导学生重新阅读文本，关注文本中的 Scott 日记部分，从中推断出在回程时 Scott 队伍中队员们的情绪变化，并提供相应依据。在小组讨论中探讨 Scott 探险精神的内涵。

2. 随后，继续追问学生：在当时条件下，Scott 队伍做出了什么样的选择，是放弃还是继续前进？他们为什么要带着 20 公斤的石头前行？难道他们不知道这样会加重自己的负担吗？

3. 组织学生讨论：In the text，Scott and his team are regarded as heroes. Do you agree with the writer's opinion? What makes them heroes? 结合学生的发言，教师最后总结：Scott 队伍的

英雄主义在于他明知道前方危险不断仍然义无反顾,敢为他人所不为,从“负重 20 公斤石头前行”可以看出来他们此行并不纯粹是为了自己,更是为了人类福祉。

4. 引导学生思考如何理解标题中的 race 一词,并组织学生进行小组讨论。race 不仅仅是表面意义上的竞赛,更是人与自然的竞赛、生与死的竞赛。

本活动中问题的答案来源于课文,但不在文章表面,需要学生进行推理、归纳、想象、判断,能够锻炼学生的思维能力。本文体现了 Scott 坚定不移的信念、超常的勇气以及甘愿为科学研究献身等英雄特质,使 Scott 的英雄主义更加立体。本活动起到主旨升华的重要作用。基于前文对 Scott 队伍的品质探索,此处教师应引导学生思考人与自然的关系,回应阅读活动中对文章标题的探讨,带领学生由表及里地理解文章标题中 race 的含义,使文章的中心思想及本单元 Human and Nature 的主题更加突出。

Activity 4:Analysis and evaluation

作业 1:Make a poster about Scott's journey to the Antarctica and include your personal feelings for his journey.

引导学生评价历史人物,思考人与自然的关系。学生课后完成海报制作。

作业 2:仿照本文的正序写作手法,结合校园篮球赛活动写一篇记叙文,描述比赛的过程,体现参赛球员们的拼搏精神。

(四)技巧归纳

故事情节和事件的叙述,最关键的是要做到条理清晰、纹丝不乱,每个事件发生的时间都有准确的描述,事件发生的先后顺序更不能混乱。在叙述中要善于使用各种时间状语,比如:副词 soon、then、later、finally、afterwards、initially;短语 one day、a few days later、shortly after、to begin with、in the end、within hours、at first、by the end of、six months ago、the final thing;介词 on、at、in、during、over;时间状语从句 when…、until…、before…、after…、since…等。很多动词也可以用来表示事情发展的时间顺序,比如:start to do/doing、end up、begin with、set about doing sth、come to an end 等。

(五)迁移创新

回顾自己的生活,同学们一定经历过很多特别难忘的第一次,比如第一次旅行、第一次做饭、第一次在实验室里做实验、第一次照顾生病的家人等。请同学们回忆自己生活中的经历,与同伴进行分享,然后创作初稿。注意恰当使用和时间相关的表达,详细描述当时都发生了什么。

（六）作品舞台

学生作品 1

Last year, I went to Guang Zhou in the summer vacation. I felt so excited. It took me about four hours to get there. In the daytime, the air was so stuffy and the sun was so hot, so my friends and I decided to take a rest in the hotel. When the sun almost got down, we started to go on the street; the first thing was to find something to eat. There were so many delicious snacks, we had no idea which to eat, so we planned to eat as much as we could. I found myself couldn't stop eating, the food was tasty. After we finishing eating, we started to go shopping. Guang Zhou is famous for the foreign trade, its clothes are fashionable and cheap. We went to the shopping street, trying on all kinds of clothes. At last, we bought many clothes. This trip is so unforgettable to me.

教师点评：

这篇文章在叙述自己去广州旅行的经历时条理分明，时间线清晰，恰当地使用了表示时间的句子和短语，比如 When the sun almost got down、the first thing was to find something to eat、After we finishing eating、At last。但是文中也存在一些语言错误和需要修改完善的表达方式，比如："There were so many delicious snacks, we had no idea which to eat, so we planned to eat as much as we could. I found myself couldn't stop eating, the food was tasted."这两句话可以使用状语从句结构分别进行简化合并，改为："There were so many delicious snacks that we had no idea which to eat. The food was so tasty that we couldn't stop eating."这样表达就显得更加流畅、紧凑。"Guang Zhou is famous for the foreign trade, its clothes are fashionable and cheap."这句话的句子结构存在错误，可以改为："Guang Zhou is famous for foreign trade, with a variety of fashionable and cheap clothes."

学生作品 2

This summer holiday, I went to Dalian with my family. We got there by air. Dalian is a very beautiful and modern city. On the bus, we could see all kinds of buildings which were great.

In the morning, we got to the hotel where we lived. After breakfast, we began our travel. First, we took the bus to the Sea Park. There are so many different kinds of fishes that I couldn't believe my eyes. We also saw the show of dolphins. Then we had lunch in a restaurant. The seafood which was very famous in China was delicious. After lunch we went swimming. The sea was blue and beach was golden. We all enjoyed ourselves in the sea. Finally, we went back the hotel where we lived. We had a happy day. In this trip, we also went to some places which were interesting and famous in Dalian, going shopping and so on.

Several days later, we left Dalian. On our way home, we were very happy. This was the reason why we didn't feel tired. In all, we had a good holiday.

学生互评：

这篇文章使用了较多的时间表达，比如 In the morning、After breakfast、First、Then、After lunch、Finally、Several days later 等，显得先后顺序非常清楚。但是也有一些错误，比如 The sea was blue and beach was golden 这句话里，beach 前面应该有冠词 the。we went back the hotel where we lived 这句话里面 back 后面漏写了 to。另外，第二段结尾处的 We had a happy day 和第三段中的 we were very happy 表达的意思比较重复，稍显啰嗦，建议都合并到结尾段。

二、注重衔接，逻辑清晰

（一）类别解析

英语语言表达比较重视句子与句子之间的衔接。相比之下，汉语表达整体上比较含蓄，常常是“言有尽而意无穷”，需要读者根据语境体会文章中句子之间的逻辑关系。不同于汉语的“意合”，英语注重的是“形合”，即在语言表达形式上，大量使用表达上下句之间意思和逻辑关系的衔接词，使句子与句子之间连贯通顺、表意清晰，不容易产生歧义。在写作中，我们要注意到英语表达的这个特点，根据句子之间的逻辑关系，比如因果、递进、转折、解释、举例等，使用合适的衔接词来增加文章的连贯性，使叙述更加流畅。

（二）精研文本

新剑桥第五册第三单元 Read and Listen 板块的文章讲述的是一个 28 岁的英国喜剧演员 Danny Wallace 如何建立起一个名为 Lovely 的国家的过程。为了使 Lovely 成为一个真正的国家，Danny Wallace 做了大量的前期筹备工作。作者在描述他的准备工作时，是如何把一件件事情叙述得清晰又有条理的呢？我们来看文章中的例子：

So, naming himself King Danny Ⅰ and declaring his one-bedroom flat in East London an independent state, he set about taking the necessary steps to make his dream come true. …

Over the six weeks, Danny explored the practicalities of forming your own country. **The first thing** on his agenda was to hand in his Declaration of Independence to the prime minister at Number Ten. **With this out of the way**, he was free to start thinking about things such as writing a constitution and setting up a government. **Then** he was off to design his own flag and record his own national anthem. He **even** got someone to design possible postage stamps for Lovely, with his face on them!

… He **also** took advice from a cardinal at the Vatican, and from the linguist and philosopher Noam Chomsky on the nature of democracy. **After** a trip to Death Row in the USA and a moving interview with an inmate, Danny decided against the death penalty for Lovely.

For economic advice, Wallace visited the chief cashier of the Bank of England. He decided to create a brand new currency, which he called the *Independent Occupational Unit* (IOU). **However**, you can't open a bank account or take out a loan in Lovely…

… **Unfortunately**, his request was ultimately turned down because of his lack of an independent territory. **Although** Danny had bought his flat, he had not purchased the land on which it stands, **so** officially his headquarters belonged to the UK. **But** what disappointed Danny most of all was being refused entry to the Eurovision Song Contest…

The final thing Danny had to do was to find a name for his country…

文章中使用的这些衔接词不仅使文章显得更加连贯,让我们看到Danny在有条不紊、一步一步地实现自己建立一个真正国家的梦想,同时,文中even、also、however、unfortunately、although、but这些衔接词的使用也让我们感受到Danny在实现梦想的道路上所做出的巨大努力和遇到的各种意想不到的困难与挫折,从而让我们看到Danny的热情、投入和执着,明白任何梦想的实现都不是一帆风顺的,需要克服重重困难并付出巨大的努力。

新剑桥第四册第十四单元中的*School of Rock*是一篇电影梗概介绍。该电影讲述的是一个穷困潦倒却依然热爱摇滚的青年Dewey在摇滚梦屡屡受挫、生活几近走投无路的情况下,顶替室友到一所小学冒充老师,带领一群10岁的孩子组建乐队并参加选秀比赛的喜剧故事。文章第一段是故事背景介绍:

It stars Jack Black as Dewey, a guitarist who won't give up his dream of living a rock'n'roll lifestyle. **But** in the real world of overdue rent and his flatmate Ned's nagging girlfriend, it's becoming almost impossible to achieve. **However**, Dewey has a plan—to win a $20,000 talent contest with his band. **Unfortunately**, the other band members decide that his on-stage clowning is embarrassing and that they have a better chance of winning without him. **So** one day Dewey arrives at rehearsal to find that the band has a new guitarist.

作者使用了but、however、unfortunately、so这些衔接词来描述电影主人公Dewey当时的处境,不仅使叙述前后衔接紧密,更突出了Dewey一边怀揣着摇滚梦,一边要面对现实的残酷:一直拖欠的房租、抛弃自己的乐队队友。这些衔接词的使用生动描写出了被现实无情捶打的Dewey所面临的诸事不利的窘迫处境。

(三)课例展示

教材:新剑桥第三册第九单元

文本分析：本单元以流传甚广却真假难辨的一些热门传闻和神秘的动物学研究发现为话题，使学生学会区分“观点”和“事实”，培养学生的批判性思维。阅读部分由两个文本 Text A 和 Text B 组成，都是关于发生在美国空军罗斯威尔基地的外星人事件。有趣的是，两篇文章中事件的目击者对于事件给出了完全不同的描述。本文提供了非常好的阅读素材，帮助学生练习在面对自相矛盾的信息时，学会思考问题并通过对信息进行分析来做出判断，辨别真伪。在这节课中，每个学生都需要通过有目的的阅读、提问、交流和讨论，最终获得自己想要的信息，发现事实的真相。这正是这个单元的标题 The Truth Is Out There 所要教给我们的。

文章叙述了 1947 年初次报道罗斯威尔事件时和 1978 年该事件再次获得人们关注时，基地军官和一些目击者在接受采访中给出的自相矛盾、前后不一的各种说法。为了把这些时隔 30 余年的扑朔迷离的信息清晰且有条理地展现出来，文章使用了大量衔接词：

On 8th July, 1947, an army officer reported a crash at the Roswell base in New Mexico, USA. **Although** the area was an air field, the details of the crash sounded strange… They said there were pieces of UFO at the base. **But** later the same day, other army officers denied the UFO story… **Even though** some officers said they had seen bodies of aliens shortly after the crash, few believed the UFO story…

However, in 1978 the story appeared again when a UFO expert interviewed some people… Several of them still said it couldn't have been a UFO that crashed. **But** one man disagreed… **Slowly**, other witnesses started agreeing with him, saying there were bodies of aliens hidden at the base.

In spite of investigations, we still don't know what really happened on that day in 1947.

教学目标

1. 通过自学和小组学习来训练学生的阅读能力；

2. 学习新单词，并在交流和演示中进行应用：crash、deny、wreckage、witness、evidence、alien、investigation；

3. 在小组活动中通过提问和回答，复述课文并发表意见，训练口语能力；

4. 学会分析获得的信息，并通过批判性思维形成自己的观点。

教学重点

1. 帮助学生练习阅读能力，以全面理解课文的内容和细节；

2. 激发学生的兴趣，激励他们积极参与课堂活动；

3. 鼓励学生清晰、有逻辑地形成和陈述自己的观点。

教学步骤)))

Activity 1：Lead-in

让学生看课本上的图片，猜猜是什么。这一步是为了激发学生的好奇心，使其集中注意力。然后，通过提问来鼓励他们谈论不明飞行物，以引起他们的兴趣。

在谈论不明飞行物和外星人时，用图片和例子教授新单词。图片有助于解释新单词的含义，使学生更容易理解。

Activity 2：Reading

告诉学生，他们将阅读关于同一事件的两篇不同的课文。首先，把全班分成两组：A 组和 B 组。

1）Individual work

要求 A 组只阅读文本 A，B 组只阅读文本 B。学生各自阅读课文，并在自己的纸上回答问题。这一步是让学生阅读课文并对其有一个大致的了解。

A 组学生

阅读第 68 页的文本 A，并回答以下问题：

What happened at the Roswell base on 8th July, 1947?

What did some officers see at the time of the crash?

Very few believed it was a UFO crash. Why was that?

What did the witness say when another crash happened in 1978 again?

B 组学生

阅读第 126 页的文本 B，并回答以下问题：

Why was the witness (his friend) surprised when he first saw the wreckage?

What did they do to the wreckage of the crash?

What did the witness say he and his friends saw?

2）Group work

完成后，让学生在小组内检查答案。然后，让他们完成表格上的课文摘要，并试着在小组内复述发生了什么。这一步是鼓励学生在这个过程中与他人合作并互相帮助。

A 组学生

在小组内检查答案，并根据文本 A 谈论发生了什么。

合上书，一起完成课文摘要。

Roswell was a/an __________ in New Mexico. When the crash happened, people from the base thought what they found were __________. But later, they __________ the UFO story and believed it was the __________ of a balloon because ____________________. However, a UFO expert interviewed __________ of the crash and some of them said the officers had hidden__________ __________ at the base.

B 组学生

在小组内检查答案，并根据文本 B 谈论发生了什么。

合上书，一起完成课文摘要。

When the crash happened at the Roswell Army Air Field, people from the base expected to see __________. However, the officers later said it was a/an __________ and many people believed the story because at that time the base was __________ other countries with balloons. But what surprised a UFO expert was that an officer working at the base said he saw __________ and that the wreckage was from a __________, which was __________ __________ by the base shortly after the crash.

3) Inter-group communication

让学生与另一组的学生一起讨论，向他/她询问他/她读过的内容，以了解更多关于这一事件的信息。

When and where did the crash happen?

What did people see at the time of the crash?

What did they believe what they found was?

Who believes the witness?

…

这一步是为学生提供一个真正的交流理由：获得他们需要的更多信息，让学生有更多机会练习口语。

Activity 3: Group discussion

让学生与另一组的学生一起讨论罗斯威尔是否发生了不明飞行物坠毁事件。要求他们用文本中的信息和从他人那里获得的信息来支撑自己的论点。

Activity 4: Presentation

让两组学生清楚地陈述他们对实际发生的事情的看法，使用文本中的词汇和信息来支撑自己的论点。

Activity 5: Reflection

激发学生思考我们是否应该相信我们所看到的，如谚语"眼见为实"所说。

（四）技巧归纳

在记叙文写作中，要注意使用衔接词为文章润色。根据句间的逻辑关系，衔接词可以分为以下几大类：

因果关系：therefore、thus、so、as a result、as a result of、because、since、now that、on account of、because of、consequently、thanks to、owing to、in order to、so that、so as to；

并列关系：and、also、as well as、both… and…、either… or…、neither… nor…、in the same way, too；

转折关系：however、but、though、although、however、nevertheless、while；

对比关系：by contrast、in comparison with、compared with、as… as…、more than、on the contrary；

递进关系：in addition、not only… but also…、besides、what's more、even worse、additionally、moreover、furthermore；

举例：for example、for instance、take… for example、such as、just like；

解释说明：that is、that is to say、in other words、or rather、to be exact。

（五）迁移创新

回忆高中生活中你曾经遇到的困难，以 *How I Overcame the Difficulty* 为题目写一篇记叙文，描述你是如何克服和战胜困难的。

（六）作品舞台

学生作品 1

My parents are very busy with their work and we have little time to talk. When I tell them things at school, they just won't listen. As a result, we talk less with each other, which makes me very upset. One day, I came across a lecture by an expert on how to communicate with others and realized that I should take a more active attitude. Therefore, I try to tell them my feelings and ideas in a calm way. Although we can't reach an agreement every time and even argue sometimes, I'm happy that we communicate more often and understand each other better now.

教师点评：

文章从遇到的困难、困难产生的原因、如何找到解决办法、采取何种措施几个方面详细叙述了自己克服困难学会沟通的经历，语言流畅，叙事条理清晰。但是注意，文章的前面部分应使用过去时态。

学生作品 2

I used to be a top student in junior high school. But when I entered senior high school, I was no longer the top one. In spite of all my efforts, I could hardly finish the homework and felt very tired every day. I didn't know what I can do to improve or whether I can make it. Fortunately, my headteacher helped me when I needed it most. Mr Zheng showed me the importance of making plans and how to make better use of my study time. Besides, he also told me to listen to the teachers in class carefully always came first. Thanks to Mr. Zheng, I'm gradually making progress now. I'm confident that if I keep on working hard, I will be a top student again.

学生互评：

文章非常真实，写出了高中生入学之初遇到的学业困难和逐渐艰难适应的过程，并写出了克服困难的方法和决心。语言表达方面，作者用了很多恰当的衔接词，使文章很连贯，但个别地方有语法错误。

三、报告文学，生动感人

（一）类别解析

报告文学(literary journalism)是一种介于新闻报道和文学作品之间的文体，其题材和所描写的人物是真实发生的历史事件和真实人物。报告文学和普通新闻报道的最大区别在于，前者对事件发生的环境和所涉及的人物有生动的描绘，并运用多种修辞方法来组织语言，更能激发读者的情感，从而打动读者。

（二）精研文本

人教版新教材必修第一册第四单元的课文 *The Night the Earth Didn't Sleep* 是一篇报告文学，主要让学生了解 20 世纪 70 年代的唐山大地震。文章虽然没有报告文学中常见的中心人物，但是按照地震前、地震中、地震后的顺序描述了唐山大地震这场灾难。文章开篇描述了地震之前出现的一些异常景象：

Strange things were happening… the water in the village wells **rose and fell**, **rose and fell**. There were deep cracks that **appeared** in the well walls. At least one well had some smelly gas **coming out of it**. Chickens and even pigs were **too nervous to eat**, and dogs **refused to go inside** buildings. Mice **ran out of the fields** looking for places to hide, and fish **jumped out of the water**. At about 3:00 a.m., on 28 July 1976, **bright lights** were seen in the sky outside the city of Tangshan and **loud noises** were heard.

本段第一句即是总起句，之后的句子使用了较多动词，语言生动，富有画面感，营造出一种重大事件发生前的紧张氛围。

第二、三段着力刻画了大地震发生时的骇人场景以及地震发生后满目疮痍、让人绝望的画面：

At 3:42 a.m., everything began to shake. It seemed **as if the world were coming to an end!** Eleven kilometers directly below the city, **one of the most deadly earthquakes** of the 20th century had begun, a quake that even **caused damage** more than **150 kilometers** away in Beijing. Nearly *one third of the whole nation felt it!* **A huge crack, eight kilometers long and 30 meters wide, cut across houses**, roads, and waterways. Hard hills of rock became **rivers of dirt.** In less than one minute, a large city **lay in ruins.** Two thirds of the people who lived there were **dead or injured.** Thousands of children were left **without parents.** The number of people who were killed or badly injured in the quake was **more than** 400,000.

Everywhere survivors looked, there was **nothing but ruins.** Nearly everything in the city was **destroyed.** About **75 percent** of the city's factories and buildings, **90 percent** of its homes, and all of its hospitals **were gone.** Bricks covered the ground like red autumn leaves, but no wind could blow them away. Most bridges had **fallen** or were **not safe to cross.** The railway tracks were now **useless pieces of metal. Tens of thousands of** cows, **hundreds of thousands of** pigs, and **millions of** chickens were **dead.** Sand now filled the wells instead of water. People were **in shock**—and then, later that afternoon, another big quake shook Tangshan again. Even more buildings **fell down.** Water, food, and electricity were **hard to get.** People began to wonder how long the disaster would last.

这两段的最大特点是数字多、数据多,既有时间,也包括距离、人数、事物的数量。精确到分的时间,不仅准确描述了地震发生的过程,而且还营造出一种灾难发生时步步紧逼和让人无法喘息的紧张氛围。而其他数据的使用,则突出体现了报告文学纪实性的特点,增强了事件的真实感。

最后两段描写的是地震之后,灾区人民虽身处绝境但不放弃希望,国家和人民军队全力支持,唐山人民在废墟之上重建家园,唐山这座被自然灾害摧毁的城市重获新生:

But **hope was not lost. Soon after** the quakes, the army sent 150,000 soldiers to Tangshan to **dig out** those who were trapped and to **bury the dead.** More than 10,000 doctors and nurses came to **provide medical care.** Workers **built shelters for survivors** whose homes had been destroyed. Hundreds of thousands of people **were helped.** Water and food were **brought into the city** by train, truck, and plane. Slowly, **the city began to breathe again.**

Tangshan started to **revive itself and get back up on its feet.** With **strong support from the government** and the **tireless efforts** of the city's people, a **new Tangshan** was built upon the earthquake ruins. The new city has become a home to more than seven million people, with **great improvements** in transportation, industry, and environment. Tangshan city has proved to China and the rest of the world that in times of disaster, people must **unify and show the wisdom to**

stay positive and rebuild for **a brighter future**.

纵观全文,文章使用了很多修辞手段,除了第一段中的排比(parallelism),还有以下修辞手段:

拟人:*The Night the Earth Didn't Sleep*; Slowly, the city began to breathe again. Tangshan started to revive itself and get back up on its feet.

重复:the water in the village wells rose and fell, rose and fell.

明喻:It seemed as if the world were coming to an end! Bricks covered the ground like red autumn leaves.

暗喻:Hard hills of rock became rivers of dirt.

本单元练习册的阅读文本 *The Story of an Eyewitness* (*Adapted*)改编自美国著名作家杰克·伦敦(Jack London)的作品,也属于纪实体报告文学。该文讲述的是1906年4月18日发生的San Francisco地震及之后的大火。文章是5月5日所写,主要讲述的是地震后发生大火的情景以及人们在大火之后所表现出来的人性光辉。

文章共分四段,第一段交代背景:

San Francisco, *May* 5, 1906. The earthquake that hit San Francisco on April 18 shook down hundreds of thousands of dollars' worth of walls and chimneys (烟囱). But the fire that followed burned up hundreds of millions of dollars' worth of buildings and homes. Never before in history has a city been so completely destroyed. San Francisco is gone. The factories, the great stores and newspaper buildings, the hotels, and the great houses of the rich are all gone.

第一句通过几组对比(contrast)比较了地震和大火带来的损失:地震带来的损失是hundreds of thousands of dollars' worth,而大火带来的损失是hundreds of millions of dollars' worth,是地震带来损失的1000倍;地震损坏的是walls and chimneys,而大火摧毁的是buildings and homes。这样的对比让读者感到触目惊心。价值上的对比稍显抽象,但是后面具象的对比则更加直接和感性:墙壁、烟囱毁了可以重新堆砌,但是大楼和家园毁了则很难再建,即使再建也需要花更多的时间、精力和金钱。本文紧接着用了一个倒装句,点明历史上没有哪个城市像当时的San Francisco一样被摧毁得这么彻底。接着一个短句、一个长句,一个抽象、一个具象,告诉读者原来的那个San Francisco再也回不来了。

第二段介绍大火开始燃烧:

On Wednesday morning at a quarter past five came the earthquake. A moment later, the disaster was a fact. South of Market Street, in the working-class neighborhoods and in the factories, fires started. Within an hour of the first quake, the smoke could be seen 100 miles away. The sun was red in the dark sky. There was no stopping the fires. The firefighters to whom the task was given did their best but there was no way to organize or communicate. The railway tracks were now useless and there was no water in water pipes. All of the ways man had made to keep the city safe were gone in the 30 seconds the earth moved.

第三段的第一句用了拟人的修辞手法，是本段的中心句，由此我们可以知道，从下午到晚上，一半的市中心就消失了。

By Wednesday afternoon, half the heart of the city was gone. At that time, I watched the disaster from a ship on the bay (海湾). Out at sea it was calm. No wind came up. Yet from every direction—east, west, north, and south—strong winds blew upon the unlucky city and those whose homes had once stood in its green hills.

本段还运用了对比(contrast)的修辞。海上：平静、无风；陆上：来自四面八方的大风在狂吹城市。这恰恰也助长了大火的肆虐。

第四段的第一句也用了拟人的修辞手法，主要讲述人性的光辉。

Wednesday night saw the destruction of the very heart of the city. Man himself had to make ruins of some of the city's best buildings so that they would not be a danger to those in the streets. Tens of thousands who had lost their homes left the city to look for shelter from the fires. Some were dressed only in blankets and carried the things that they had been able to rescue from the fires. But there were no fights and no pushing or shoving. Somehow this worst of disasters brought out the best in the survivors. Never in all of San Francisco's history were her people so kind as on this night of terror.

本段前面谈到为了不造成伤害，人们不得不把大火烧成的断壁残垣全部砸掉。可以想见，把自己亲手建造起来的家园再亲手毁掉，会是怎样的心痛！但是为了他人的安危，也只能如此。后面谈到幸存者披着毯子、拿着能够抢救出来的物品逃离家园的情景，体现出文本结构中的对比关系，即“灾难的无情”(Paras. 1—3)和“人类的有情”(Para. 4)。最后一句用倒装句和通感(恐怖之夜，night of terror)的修辞手段对这种人性作了总结：这种善良是 San Francisco 历史上不曾有过的，但是在这个大火之夜却达到了巅峰。

（三）课例展示

教材：人教版新教材必修第一册第四单元 Workbook 部分的文本 *The Story of an Eyewitness* (*Adapted*)

文本分析：本文以时间顺序为明线，对比为暗线，通过大量生动的场面描写来表现自然灾害的 destruction。Lead-in 部分谈论灾难和新闻，导入话题，并通过 2004 年海啸的视频引入本篇文章的文体特征，使学生对 literary journalism 的特点有一个初步的认识。学生运用新闻概要写作技能，归纳概括文章的主要事件及时间线，了解文章的主要内容和结构，从而对文章的时间线与事件有一个框架性的认识，理解旧金山地震及经历地震的人们。教师让学生写文章的summary，对文章的主要事件进行整合，在这一过程中提升学生的概括归纳能力。同时，让学生对文本语言进行阅读与赏析，感受语言运用并学习和理解作者使用的写作手法，探究如何运用这些写作手法表达情感、创设意境，培养学生的批判性思维。学生需要对输入环节的内容进行整合、梳理，输出基于报告文学这一文体的概要写作，要做到既具有事实概述，又兼具文学特色。学生使用所学的写作手法描述各种场景，练习所学的写作手法，提升综合语言运用能力，并为输出的写作任务做铺垫。

教学目标

1. 了解新闻报道与文学新闻的区别；
2. 写一篇包含主要新闻元素的新闻摘要；
3. 学习 *The Story of an Eyewitness* 中运用的文学技巧；
4. 写一篇 *The Story of an Eyewitness* 的精简版。

教学重点

1. 掌握文章的提纲和文学技巧；
2. 写一篇 *The Story of an Eyewitness* 的精简版；
3. 运用所学的写作技巧。

教学步骤

Activity 1：Lead-in

通过观看一段印尼海啸的新闻报道和一段描述印尼海啸经历的视频，引入话题（灾难）与新闻报道这一文体，引导学生感知新闻报道与文学描述的区别，从而引入报告文学的概念及其文体特征。

Activity 2：Write a news summary

1. Get the main events.

引导学生掌握事件的主要信息：时间、地点、事件、影响以及后续事件。

2. Learn cohesion devices.

引入写作中三种主要的连接手法，并引导学生找到文本中使用的连接手法。

3. Write and present the news summary.

引导学生写出本文的概要（包括主要事件的信息）并展示；帮助学生学会使用连接手段使概要连贯。

Activity 3：Learn the literary techniques

1. Read and appreciate.

激励学生感知并探索写作手法表达的深层含义及情感，为迁移创新做准备；引导学生感知和欣赏语言的力量与美。

2. Learn and summarize.

引入本文所用的写作手法（如白描等）的概念；激励学生感知并探索写作手法在文本中的功能，理解 tell 与 show 的区别；引导学生理解好的作品具备的特征。

Activity 4：Creation

创设不同的情境，引导学生运用所学的写作手法来表达；学生分组讨论在描述图片时可以使用哪些技巧，并使用自己在本课中学到的写作技巧来描述图片，以创造生动的场景。

Activity 5：Write and present the shortened edition

完成本节课写作任务：写出本文的缩写版，完善作文并在班内展示。引导学生总结所学内容，并重申本课的主要任务，即用文学技巧撰写新闻摘要，以确保学生清楚自己的任务。学生将写一篇精简版的 *The Story of an Eyewitness*，然后对照检查表修改草稿，并提交最终稿。

Activity 6：Homework

鼓励学生在新情境中巩固和运用所学内容，改进海啸经历者对自己经历的描述。

（四）技巧归纳

报告文学是新闻报道和文学作品的有机融合，兼具真实性和文学性。不同于小说的虚构，报告文学既要忠实于事件真相，还要用文学化的语言塑造人物，并对环境进行刻画和渲染。在写作中要注意使用丰富的修辞手法，比如下面这些修辞手法。

排比（parallelism），比如“As a player, Lang Ping brought honor and glory to her country. As a coach, she led the China women's volleyball team to medals at world championships and the Olympics. As a person, Lang Ping is loved by fans at home and abroad.”；

拟人（personification），比如在谈到音乐对自己的影响时，“It became my best friend. It spoke words of encouragement to the deepest part of my being.”，在谈到唐山地震发生后开展灾后救援工作时，“Slowly, the city began to breathe again. Tangshan started to revive itself and get back up on its feet.”；

夸张（exaggeration），比如“It seemed as if the world were coming to an end!”；

重复（repetition），比如“Music gave me happiness. ... Music gave me strength and brought me relief. ... Music gave me hope and a sense of satisfaction.”；

明喻（simile），比如“When I listened to music, it made my spirits fly like a kite in the wind.""Bricks covered the ground like red autumn leaves.";

暗喻(metaphor),比如"It was the rock I leant on to become strong and to get through those hard times.""Hard hills of rock became rivers of dirt.";

对比(contrast);

引用(quote),比如"John A. Logan said, 'Music is the medicine of the mind.' And it's true. Music helped me recover.";

反问句,修辞问句(rhetorical question),比如"Have you ever faced a time when things looked dark and you had no hope at all?"。

灵活使用修辞手法有利于充分发挥语言的感染力,达到激发读者感情、引发共鸣或增强情感的目的。

同时,报告文学中还要用好细节描写,比如数字、区域范围、影响程度等都应尽可能详细准确,给读者以真实可信的感觉。

5. 迁移创新

上周多地区因降雨受到洪水灾害影响,并导致人员伤亡和经济损失。请根据以下信息写一篇新闻报道,详细描述灾情影响。

人员伤亡	7 人丧生,2 人下落不明,3 万多人受到影响,1.6 万人被疏散
造成损失	140 公顷农作物被淹,经济损失逾 3 亿,多条铁路被毁,交通停滞
救灾措施	900 多万元救灾款,数千志愿者加入救援工作

(六)作品舞台

学生作品 1

A terrible flood has left 7 people dead and 2 missing since rainstorms struck the areas last week. 16 thousand people have been evacuated to safe places. This flood is like a monster, swallowing a large piece of land and destroying 140 hectares of crops. What's more, lots of railways are ruined, lots of trains are stopped and more than 300 million worth of economic loss is caused. In spite of all the pain and suffering, these places are breathing again with the rescue operation on the way. People have raised more than 9 million to support the flooded area and thousands of volunteers have arrived to search for and rescue the trapped people. The flood is cold and cruel, but warmth and kindness in the world give us hope for a new life.

教师点评：

文章用大量翔实的数据描述了洪水给当地的人们所造成的巨大损失，同时还使用了文学修辞手法，比如"This flood is like a monster, swallowing a large piece of land and destroying 140 hectares of crops."一句把洪水比喻成吞没良田的野兽。在报道救灾行动的时候，运用对比（The flood is cold and cruel, but warmth and kindness in the world give us hope for a new life.）描绘出洪水无情人有情的温暖画面。总的来说，这是一篇语言流畅、内容翔实的新闻报道，体现出了报告文学的语言特点。

学生作品 2

Floods caused by continuous heavy rains have claimed 7 lives and left 2 people missing in the past week. Heavy rains go on to cause more destruction. Many houses and crops are washed away, many people are removed to other places, and many trains are stopped. Thousands of people lost their home, thousands of farmers lost their land, and thousands of children lost their laughter. To save people from this disaster, volunteers have joined in the rescue work. More than 9 million has been spent on rebuilding people's homes. A new sun will rise on this flood-stricken land.

学生互评：

文章基本涵盖了表格中的主要信息点，有些具体数字没有呈现。在对洪水新闻事件的报道中，使用了排比句来加强洪水所带来的严重破坏（Thousands of people lost their home, thousands of farmers lost their land, and thousands of children lost their laughter.）。

第四节　议论文

一、议论文的分类及要素

议论文是以议论为主要语言特征的一类文体，其对象经常是一些有争议的话题、事件或观点，通过议论最终达到厘清事实、拓宽思路，找到解决方法或得出结论。本章节结合不同教材中出现的议论文体及议论文写作的常见结构，将议论文大致分为驳论类、正反分析类、分析并提出己见类、提出一分析一解决问题类。正反分析类、分析并提出己见类、提出一分析一解决问题类几类合在一起亦是立论类。

从要素上来说，议论文一般包括论点、论据、论证三个要素。论点可以说是议论文的灵魂,任何一篇议论文都是围绕论点来展开的。根据展开情况,论点可能由几个分论点来进行支撑。它们相互结合,就像一棵大树的主干和分枝。论据可以说是议论文的血肉,论点需要论据进行支撑才能鲜活。论据包括事实论据、数据论据、名言警句、科学道理、专家观点等。它们具体且有说服力,使论点进一步得到确认。论证则是将论据和论点合二为一的过程,即用论据来证明论点。论证往往借助一定的逻辑,如因果、对比、类比、正反分析等。

论点、论据、论证,犹如议论文的三个轮子,它们相互作用,才能让议论文的马车开动起来。议论文的写作过程是将题目铺开、详尽分析、求同存异的过程,是从一团迷雾到云淡风轻的过程。同时,议论文的准备和写作过程对于学生思辨能力的培养也有着不容小觑的作用。

二、驳论类

(一)类别解析

驳论,顾名思义就是驳斥别人的观点,表明自己的观点。它的特点是“驳”,对学生思辨能力的培养至关重要。就批驳的形式来说,主要分为两种:第一种,针锋相对地指出对方观点和论据中的问题,进行分析和批判,进而提出自己认为合理的观点。换言之,就是一“破”二“立”;第二种,就同一话题提出自己的看法,通过论证和举例等证明自己的观点,与另一立场的一方形成势不两立的格局。换言之,就是先“立”,从而“破”。就相关性来说,驳论和辩论有十分紧密的关系。华语辩论和 BP 辩论中,选手都需要找到对立一方辩手观点及论据中的疏漏之处,从而进行批驳。如果参加辩论的学生进一步将观点进行梳理,就能形成一篇很好的驳论文。所以,培养学生驳论文的写作能力可以和辩论有机结合起来。

(二)精研文本

下面结合两本教材中的两篇此类文章,做以下分析。

首先,北师大版旧教材选修第八册第二十四单元有一篇题为 *Crime and Punishment* 的文章。该文章由两篇短文组成。

第一篇短文是一篇立论文,作者 RJ Butcher 首段先提出 Polly Filler 上周的文章写得很好,因为她谴责了对于他们国家罪犯过于温和的刑罚,然后提出自己警官哥哥提到的贩毒者和抢劫者很快就获释的现象,最后说到这种现象的后果——很多人对政府失去信心。第二段中,作者接着前面的铺垫直接提出观点:我们应该将严格的刑罚重新引入我们的国家。作者引用了美国 three strikes and out 的理念,提出在三次犯罪之后,罪犯应该终身监禁。第三段中,作者批驳了罪犯在监狱中条件优越犹如宾馆的现象,提出他们应该服劳役。第四段中,作者进一步提出应该像美国那样重新引入死刑,杀人者不配活着。

第二篇短文是一篇驳论文，作者 Paul Mason 开篇就提出 RJ Butcher 的文章骇人听闻，继而指出 RJ 观点错误的实质：把刑罚看作复仇。作者认为刑罚的首要目的是改造罪犯、使他们成为对社会有用的人。第二段中，作者开始立论：完全反对重刑，死刑应该废除。但作者也提出了一种例外情况：当罪犯一旦被释放就威胁到社会的情况下，可以使用死刑。作者认为死刑有违人类尊严，无异于谋杀，接着以列数据的形式指出美国过去 100 年中错误地处死了 23 人，另外 400 个案子也存在此种嫌疑。最后，作者指出死刑对一些社会群体不利。

此外，人教版新教材选择性必修第四册第三单元的 Using Language 部分也有两篇驳论文。

第一篇短文在第一段就以一种关切的语气提到，海洋开发已经引起了许多问题，而且还会引起更多问题：Sea exploration **has caused many** problems and will continue to **cause more**。第二段提出海洋开发造成的污染问题，并且以深水地平线石油钻井平台石油泄漏的具体案例及海洋塑料污染对鸟类、鱼类、人类饮用水的危害为例来佐证该论点。第三段提出开发海底资源造成的毁灭性后果，特别提到北极地区的例子。因为气候变化的缘故，人类可以继续往北寻觅化石能源，进而造成冰川继续融化，恶性循环由此产生。第四段提到了过度渔猎的问题。尽管 1982 年以来已经有禁令，鲸鱼和海豚或因为捕食或因为研究一直逃不脱渔猎的命运。最后一段中，作者提出海洋是所有生物的家，而非人类的私有财产，它虽然硕大但却脆弱至极，因而得出“为了后代，我们应该保护它”的结论。

第二篇短文开篇提出的第一个论点是为了真正理解我们生活的星球，我们必须开发占地颇多的海洋。作者先让步，说反对者可能是关切，继而转折说海洋开发对我们的未来至关重要，我们通过直面我们星球正在发生的事情才能采取措施应对（Opponents **may be** concerned, **but** sea exploration is important for our future）。第二段中，作者提出新的立论：对海洋更好的认识能帮我们更好地管理资源。记录新物种能促进我们对地球物种的认识，开发海洋也可能促进新药物、新食物和新能源的发现。此外，步入深海也能帮助人类预测地震这样的事件。第三段回应第一篇文章末尾的说法：人类需要开发新能源，因为世界人口一直在增长，为未来着想，我们应该开发海洋资源。最后一段，作者仍然用先让步再转折的方法回应第一篇文章中二、三两段的观点（**Of course**, there are still environmental risks. **However**, these should be balanced with economic needs.）。结尾部分，作者总结说，人类有望通过科技的进步在开发海洋资源的问题上找到一个平衡点。

（三）课例展示

教材：人教版新教材选择性必修第四册第三单元 Using Language 部分

文本分析：该部分文章的主题是“谈谈你对海洋探索的看法”。本单元中，学生通过阅读语篇了解中国从古至今探索海洋的进程，思考海洋探索对中国和世界的影响，体会“一带一路”——特别是“21 世纪海上丝绸之路”——的深远意义，通过对比两个观点相互对立的语篇来发现写作的技巧，并能学以致用。

教学目标

1. 通过阅读判断文章体裁；

2. 对比两个观点对立的议论文语篇，发现写作的技巧；

3. 通过课堂讨论，为写作的迁移进行铺垫。

教学步骤

Activity 1：Lead-in

结合本单元话题设置问题，让学生基于单元图片展开讨论，进行课堂导入。

- How much do you know about the sea?
- What adjectives would you use to describe the sea?
- Do you know any stories about sea voyages?

Activity 2：Reading

1. 学生快速阅读文章，判断语篇体裁。

What is the text type of this essay?

2. 学生分成两组，每组读一篇短文，并列出主要观点及支撑性证据。

Text 1

Exploration causes pollution.

Deepwater Horizon oil spill.

Plastic pollution.

Mining for resources is damaging.

It hurts the Arctic.

Burning fossil fuels adds to climate change.

Overfishing is an issue.

Whales and dolphins are hunted.

Banned, but some countries still do it.

Text 2

Sea exploration is important for our future.

Scientific research ships can help address important issues like climate change.

Understanding more about the sea will also help us manage its resources better.

New medicines, food resources and energy.

Predict events such as earthquakes.

We need new resources for future development.

Vast amounts of resources may be under the sea and ice.

Activity 3：Thinking and talking

学生讨论并回答以下问题。

1) What is your opinion about sea exploration? Do you agree with one argument more than the other?

2) Has your opinion changed after reading the two texts? Why or why not?

3) Are there any other aspects of sea exploration not mentioned that you think are important?

4) Have you noticed the writing skills of the two articles? Tell which chart on Page 33 can support which text. Talk about the use of Point-Evidence-Explanation-Link.

Activity 4：Writing preparation

让学生以"Is marriage across nations is good or not? /Will e-books take the place of traditional books?"为话题，分成对立的两组，发表自己的观点，并模仿阅读部分的议论文结构对自己的观点进行归纳。

Activity 5：Homework

学生以课堂讨论为依据，两两合作完成驳论文写作。

（四）技巧归纳

通过分析，我们能看出驳论文有以下技巧：

1）一针见血地指出对方观点错误的实质和主要问题，给对方以致命一击，继而提出合理的观点，即先破后立。

2）立论部分避免绝对化，提出死刑使用的一种例外情况：当罪犯一旦被释放就威胁到社会的情况下，可以使用死刑。

3）论据丰富多样，有说服力，如列出事实、摆明其中的具体数据等，增加可信性。另外，也有逻辑方面的论证，如死刑等于谋杀等，将抽象的道理有形化。

4）先让步再转折的写作手法的运用使得文章更为客观，同时新观点的提出又能极好地反驳对方观点。第二篇短文末尾寻找平衡点的说法避免了言语的直接冲突。

5）表示驳论的句型参考：

Of course,... makes sense. However, these should be balanced with...

Opponents may be concerned, but ... is more important/shouldn't be ignored/should be attached equal importance.

I oppose/object to what... says for the reason that... /on grounds that...

（五）迁移创新

对于社会热点问题，青少年普遍有着深刻的关注。随着国与国之间沟通的频繁和科技的发达，产生了一些热议的问题，如：跨国婚姻是不是更好？电子书会取代传统书吗？请选择其中一个话题，和你的同学进行思考和讨论，并写下自己的观点。

注意：作为写作前的准备，学生针对问题进行深刻的讨论，并结合课堂讨论进行立论文或驳论文的写作。此类练习可以让学生两人一组，一人先写，一人后驳，两人合作完成。

（六）作品舞台

学生作品1

Nowadays, it is easier for you to find couples across nations on the street. As far as I'm concerned, I back this phenomenon.

Reasons can be down to one key word, communication. In the first place, marriage across nations spurs the communication of different cultures. After all, some couples hit it off because unfamiliarity of languages, and hair or eye color may cause a sense of mystery and charm between them even when they are strangers. As they get to know each other further, they tend to share their own culture so that both appreciate more about each other. During this process, foreign language abilities can be boosted as well. In the second place, from a biological perspective, distance in genes adds to the possibilities of more genetic advantages for babies. It has become a consensus that persons of mixed blood are always more beautiful or handsome, which can also support my opinion.

Also, endeavors to get married have witnessed their genuine love for each other and abilities to conquer so many disputes and troubles. How can we still say no to those devoted lifelong spouses?

What should be added is that choosing a foreign spouse or not is actually a personal choice. As long as couples do not break the law or interfere with others' benefits, and take the responsibility for their chosen life path, they shouldn't be blamed or opposed. After all, it's their own lives.

学生作品2

What my partner has mentioned makes sense to a degree, but what cannot be ignored is that marriage across nations is very likely to bring conflicts. Different nationalities mean different culture backgrounds, and different culture backgrounds nurture different mindsets, which is what we call the "culture gap". This kind of gap is quite difficult to overcome, which is why so many people—my predecessors and I—choose to major in language and culture. Harmonious marriages need, from my point of view, not only charm, communication, but more importantly, common views on life. But people with different mindsets can hardly make it. Divergences and conflicts occur easily when people from two nations decide to live together, as is like a war of two nations.

Genetic advantages are one thing that amazes us superficially, but marriage across nations means the kids will lack a sense of belonging. With parents or even hometowns of different nationalities, the second generation of such families can feel really confused about which one is his mother culture, and therefore has the problem concerning the sense of belonging.

In short, problems occur in marriages across nations both for the couple and the children, so I don't agree with them.

教师点评：

第一位同学对于异国婚姻很有自己的见解，比如能促进文化交流、提升语言能力、后代基因更具优越性等。虽然是青少年，对社会问题已能提出系统的、独到的见解。最后部分的阐述，另一半的选择是个人选择问题，无所谓对错，更显示了思维的辩证性。

第二位同学反驳第一位同学的观点，主要的论点一是异国婚姻可能会带来矛盾，这跟第一位同学提出的异国婚姻中的相互吸引和交流是针锋相对的。论点二主要针对后代的归属感问题，这跟第一位同学提出的后代基因优越性等美好蓝图又形成了矛盾。第二位同学还很巧妙地两次运用了先让步后反驳的技巧，而且将异国婚姻中的矛盾冲突比作两个国家的战争，使抽象的道理具体化。

学生作品 3

There is no denying that e-books have gained increasing popularity in the past years along with the development of information technology. Taking a look around, we can find examples too numerous to list. Actually, modern readers seem to spend more time on e-books as opposed to on traditional ones.

As a consequence, it has emerged as a hotly debated topic whether e-books will take the place of traditional books in the future. I claim that it is natural for books to become electronic as mankind steps into a digital age. Compared with traditional books, e-books have some obvious advantages. For one thing, it is convenient to read on line as modern people have easy access to the Internet. For another, reading e-books saves money, facilitates mass culture and enlarges the circle of readers.

To conclude, I will arrive at the conclusion that e-books are a natural product of the digital era. We should follow the trend of the times, shouldn't we?

学生作品 4

It is universally acknowledged that, with the Internet technology updating at a stunning rate, e-books are becoming the very choice when it comes to reading. Indeed, at the age of technology, our lifestyle is altering constantly and e-books cater to the needs of times. Though e-books are stretching their sphere of influence, traditional books should not be overtaken.

First and foremost, it's indeed obvious that e-books play a crucial part in learning and are convenient. But isn't reading traditional books equally convenient and more environmentally friendly? Supposing you read a paper book in a busy subway station, you will attract numerous admirers and promote mass culture as well. Meanwhile, traditional books are a comfort for nostalgic people. On feeling the delight of touching books, memories of one's childhood flood back.

Thus, as a symbol of the golden old days, traditional books should be attached greater importance to in the digital era rather than be substituted by modern devices.

教师点评：

第四位同学针锋相对地辩驳第三位同学的观点，提出传统书阅读也一样方便，而且更加环保。这在一定程度上肯定了前者的观点，显得更加客观，但同时又强调了传统书更胜一筹，如它们一样可以推动大众文化，而且对于怀旧的人而言，传统书更是抚慰心灵、重回童年的灵汤妙药。第四位同学在结论段再次强调自己的观点，这与第三位同学在结论段提出的问题遥相呼应，针尖对麦芒，各显春秋。

三、正反分析类

（一）类别解析

事物往往是两面的，这决定了驳论的合理性，也决定了人们在看问题的时候往往会一分为二地进行分析。正反分析类议论文就像是分别展示了一个硬币的两个面，两个方面分析之后，作者往往会亮明自己的立场。

在此类文章的首段，作者往往会先以吸引人心的故事、名言、事例等将读者带入话题的情境中，使读者对话题有一个自己的预设。接着，或顺理成章，或话锋一转，提出文章的话题。接下来的两段或分析利弊，或分析事物矛盾的两个维度，一般都会辅以论证分析、事例等来证明两个方面的论点。尾段中，作者或者两者取其一，或者站中间立场，也可能会进一步阐述自己的原因或想法。

（二）精研文本

下面结合人教版新教材选择性必修第一册第二单元中一篇题为 *Should We Fight New Technology*？的议论文做以下分析。

在第一段中，作者以自己在报纸上看到的一篇报道作为引入。这篇报道是关于乘客乘坐无人驾驶的车辆遭遇交通事故的。作者谈到了大众对此事件的看法：科技上的进步是不必要而且危险的（They said that some advances in technology were **unnecessary** and **could even** be dangerous.）。因此，作者说我们不应再仅因科技之新就接受它（**Hence**，we **should** cease accepting technology **just because** it is new.）。作者继续引用，提到报纸报道说汽车公司已经就此次事件致歉，但逝者的家人觉得这样做还不够，而汽车公司坚持说不久后的将来大部分的人都会乘坐无人驾驶汽车。

第二段中，作者首句运用了中心句，提到世界上许多群体在没有高科技的情况下仍然能幸福生活。作者援引的例子是阿米什人（the Amish）：他们没车也不驾车，不看电视，不用网络，从 18 世纪以来以及很可能到漫漫未来都主要过着农耕生活。他们生活简朴，注重辛劳、家庭、社区，并且觉得这胜过追求奢华或者富人、名人的生活。作者最后一句折射出了自己的态度：应该说，阿米什人的生活质量更好，因为他们沉浸在大自然的怀抱中并得以滋养，这比居住在污染横行的大城市更惬意。结合目前人们快节奏、高压力的生活环境，阿米什人的生活场景明显具有打动人心的说服力。

第三段中，作者提到近些年高科技给各地的人们提供了许多好处，并举出例子：最近的天气追踪计算机程序使人们提前得到自然灾害的预警，使许多生命免于危险。网络使在地球两端的亲人朋友能轻松联络，也使生活中增添了许多良机，因为人们可以通过社交媒体创造更大的朋友圈。作者的分析很有条理，从 for example 的举例，到 moreover 的进一步列举，步步深入，与上一段的论述遥相呼应。

最后一段中，作者说到自己也是科技进步的受益者：自己 AI 设计师的工作是通过社交网络获得的。他（她）实时佩戴的健康检测器使自己的健康状况达到最优。作者也提到在高科技带来生活方式变革的同时，也有着令人害怕的前景，但自己仍然愿意看到它积极的一面而接受它，而不是一味抗拒（**Nevertheless**，I will always look on the positive side of change and accept it rather than resist it.）。这种以自己或普通人为例子的论证方式在人教版新教材中还是颇为常见的。

（三）课例展示

教材：人教版新教材选择性必修第一册第二单元文本 *Should We Fight New Technology*？

文本分析：该文本反映的是新时代背景下产生的科技与传统生活的矛盾。作者以头条新闻和自身经历为起点，深入探讨了该话题，既有历史的纵深感，又有地域的广阔感。经过深刻的论述，学生对话题的理解更加透彻。

教学目标

1. 阅读并理解文章的篇章结构；
2. 总结文章正反两个方面论述的写作技巧。

教学步骤

Activity 1: Lead-in

比较过去和现在的不同交通方式。现代便利往往伴随着潜在的风险。你认为我们应该对抗新技术吗?

Activity 2: Read for general idea

让学生阅读文章,找出文章的主旨大意。

Activity 3　Read for structure

分析作者如何证明主题句,并找出每段的结构。

Para. 1—introduction: a specific issue + different opinions

Para. 2 & Para. 3—the disadvantages and advantages of technology: topic sentence + supporting details

Para. 4—the author's opinion: topic sentence + example + personal experience

Activity 4: Read for language features

根据文本的结构和语言特征,找出其结构和体裁。注意作者在为这些想法辩护时使用的写作技巧。

Activity 5: Discussion

复习议论文写作的结构和要点,鼓励学生讨论探索宇宙的利弊。

Activity 6: Homework

写一篇类似的文章,谈谈宇宙探索的利弊。

(四)技巧归纳

通过分析,我们能看出上述文章有以下技巧:

1)引入新鲜事件,多维度谈论人们的看法,增加读者对话题的浸入式思考。作者在第一段中引入事件,并相应提出大众观点、汽车公司的态度,能很好地从多维度反映人们对无人驾驶车辆前景的思考。同时,以此事件作为导入,也能很好地打开新科技是否应该被接受这个话题。

2）正反两个维度进行论述，体现思维的条理性和辩证性。在二、三段中，作者进行了正反两个方面的论述，具体翔实。

3）论据具体有趣、丰富多样，容易使读者信服，同时群体的例子更有说服力。

4）讲述自己观点时提到了自己确实受益的几个具体方面，拉近和读者的距离，增加可信度；同时客观地看待问题，提出问题本身的两面性，最后亮明自己的立场。

5）正反分析类论述句型参考：

A majority of people approve of the opinion that… From their point of view, there are two factors contributing to this, which are as follows: In the first place, … Furthermore, …

On the contrary, some people differ in their opinions on this matter, arguing/claiming that… On the one hand, there are… On the other hand, … advocate/oppose…

Some people suggest/think/maintain/hold the opinion that…

Those who advocate/are in favor of… believe that…

Those who criticize/object to/oppose… maintain that…

（五）迁移创新

随着社会的发展，我们不得不面对一些争议性的问题，例如：人类是否可以开发宇宙？作为青少年，对此你的观点是什么？请就该话题与同学展开讨论，并写一篇题为 *Should We Explore the Universe?* 的作文。

注意：可以让学生在课堂上进行讨论，搜集资料，再进行写作。

（六）作品舞台

学生作品 1

With the successful launch of satellites and astronauts visiting the universe more frequently, humans are filled with extreme joy. Admittedly, this is a huge step for the entire human race, but the question of whether we should explore the universe has been controversial since the day humans set foot on the moon.

On the one hand, by exploring the universe, we know more about the origin of the planets and humans. Consequently, ample predictions about the fate of the earth are made. *The Wandering Earth* by Liu Cixin clearly exhibits our concern for our mother earth. It spurs people's thoughts about potential disasters confronting the earth and possible solutions. Besides, given the limited space, it's likely that the universe might offer alternative breeding grounds for humans.

On the other hand, exploring the universe brings problems. Space debris is intriguing to humans though it is not directly visible. And who knows whether our footsteps on other planets will bring intergalactic wars or not?

As far as I'm concerned, it's time to pay more efforts to exploring our mind rather than the universe. There are so many people, especially young ones, attracted by the cyberspace. Rather than continuously show them science epics in universe exploration, I prefer to guide them out of the marsh of the negative nihilism. Stars have shone for so long and will shine in the future. However, we just have a mortal life, which means time for us to find our sense of being is not much. Now, friends, let's get our gaze at the sky back and pay more attention on how to be a man.

教师点评：

作者以卫星、航天员的升空作为文章开头，很容易将读者带入话题，因为近年来我国航天事业取得了很多辉煌的成就。这也模仿了教材首段的技巧。接着，作者从正反两个方面分析，一方面提到了开发太空的好处，如激发人们对于地球及宇宙未来的思考，如提到《流浪地球》，另一方面又提出了自己的一些担心，如太空垃圾和星球大战。最后，作者就自己的观点进行了论述，提出我们应该更多地关注一些实际的事情，将有限的生命用于这些方面。一般来讲，对于该问题人们的态度倾向于应该开发宇宙，但作者能另辟蹊径，展开自己的论证，体现了思维的创新性。

学生作品 2

Looking back on what we have done in recent centuries, we can easily find that we have kept spreading humankind's voices and footsteps to more places in the universe. As far as I'm concerned, it's time to know more about the universe and find solutions to the earth's problems.

On the one hand, let's think about what the universe can give us: materials, physical laws and wonders. But can it provide answers to where humans can go in the future? Some vital questions can only be solved by exploring the universe and forecasting the future of the mankind. The competition among countries will be the one concerning the path of future development. And the space will without doubt be a golden field in a century or so.

On the other hand, space exploration may consume a lot of energy and money. This calls for the support of the government and strong economy. Given the post-pandemic economy, maybe it is not so urgent. And the uncertainty of economic input may worry many people to some extent. But I, a student, would like to do whatever I can to support space exploration.

Personally, I would say it's the worry that stops us from going ahead. I highly recommend adequate money and resources be applied to the realm of space exploration.

教师点评：

本文能客观公正地从正反两方面进行分析，体现了辩证的思维，同时这些观点也是生活中比较常见的保守和激进的两类观点，分析客观到位。文中作者提到自己作为普通学生也愿意为太空探索付出自己的一份力量，体现了以自己的处境作为论据的写作手法。文章最后，作者从对两种观点的分析中得出了自己的结论。

四、分析并提出己见类

（一）类别解析

该类文体内容常是针对某一问题、现象或者观点进行分析，并表明自己的观点。常见的有两种行文结构：一是针对该问题、现象或观点直接表明自己的立场，而后进行分析论证，最后再次重申，呼应开头；二是针对该问题、现象或观点，分点、分段进行详细论述、分析，在综合分析现存问题或者观点之后，最终表明自己的立场。练习此类作文可以培养学生的思辨能力和解决问题的能力。

（二）精研文本

针对结构一，首先以新剑桥第三册第四单元写作部分的课文 *Will Computers Ever Be More Intelligent than People*? 为例进行分析。

文章第一段引入话题，并表明作者的观点，即作者不赞成计算机等同或超越人类的观点（This is a **fascinating** idea, **but** I don't believe it will really happen.）。第二段从正面肯定科学家伟大的发明创造，指出计算机作为其中之一代替人类做了很多工作，且的确具备强大的记忆储备能力，正面罗列计算机的优势所在（implant tiny chips in people's brains, develop computers that can understand many things that people say, enormous memory capacities）。第三段从反面论证，指出人类的能力不局限于记忆储备功能，计算机优势虽多、功能虽强，但人类的情感交互能力是计算机所不具备的，从而有力地支撑了作者自己的观点。最后一段进行总结，再次重申作者的观点：即使计算机的能力不断发展，但依旧无法超越人类（I believe human intelligence will always be higher than artificial intelligence.）。文章每一段的第一句皆是该段的主旨句，文章内在逻辑天成。第二段的内容是为第三段进行有力反驳做铺垫，即作者不赞成该观点，从该观点所基于的基础来进行反驳，有理有据，说服力强。

再如人教版新教材必修第二册第三单元中题为 *Stronger Together*: *How We Have Been Changed by the Internet* 的文章。作者在第一段先引入话题，举例说明网络带给我们的便捷，接着提出了自己的观点："But the Internet has done much more for people than simply make life more convenient. People's lives have been changed by online communities and social networks." 接下来，作者通过 Jan Tchamani 的具体事例来论证自己的观点。她在生重病失去工作之后借助网络摆脱无聊和无尽的孤独，然后加入一个网络群体并从中获得他人的支持和建议。不仅如此，Jan 还创立了 IT 俱乐部，帮助一位 59 岁的老人网上求职并获得一份工作，帮助一位61岁的老人创办网络公司，开设网课教老年人如何使用网络，进而消除数字鸿沟，等等。这些生动的事例为作者观点的论证增加了许多可信性，因为平凡人的故事更是我们生活中的日常。

针对结构二，首先以北师大版旧教材选修模块七第二十一单元的课文 *Should People in Comas Be Kept on Life Support Machines*? 为例进行分析。

文章第一段引入话题，阐述了近期的一个热点话题，即一位美国女士 Terri Schiavo 因陷入昏迷十五年，其丈夫向法院申请停止使用生命维持仪器并最终胜诉，该女士的父母持反对意见，认为自己女儿的昏迷是暂时的。同时作者也罗列了现存的两种观点，一种认为生命是神圣的，不应被剥夺；另一种支持昏迷者丈夫的决定，认为昏迷者本人也不想这样靠机器维持生命。第二段中作者简要介绍了 Terri Schiavo 陷入昏迷的原因、昏迷者的生理状态和医学界对该类症状的认识，指出昏迷者的昏迷时间越长，恢复神智的可能性越小，因此，Terri 长达15年的昏迷状态也说明了她醒来的可能性微乎其微。第三段进一步介绍了陷入昏迷者恢复正常的几率问题。第四段作者表明自己的观点，即同意法院及医疗机构的决定，病人亲属有权决定是否停止使用生命维持仪器，但前提是病人已接受所能提供的治疗，的确是无望恢复。课文首段引入话题并陈述现存观点，第二、三两段对话题本身做出分析，为最后一段表明自己的观点做支撑。

除此之外，我们再来看看人教版新教材选择性必修第一册第五单元中一篇题为 *Chemical Versus Organic Farming* 的文章。该文章的第一段先引出话题："Chemical pesticides and artificial fertilisers **have been in widespread use in farming since** the middle of the 20th century."之后按照时间顺序，说明它们的使用状况："**When they were first introduced**, ... **Over time, however, what some scientists have found is that** their long-term use can sometimes harm both the land and people's health."该句也提出了作者所论述的观点。第二段中，作者通过举例，说明杀虫剂会杀害有害的和有益的细菌和昆虫，停留在泥土和地下的化学物质影响到作物，使作物外表好看但缺乏营养，进而影响到人类的健康。第三、四段中，作者从有机农业的角度来分析，介绍了有机农业的做法，如通过天然的方式使土壤肥沃、每年更换作物类型、套种不同作物等，这些做法都对环境有利。第五段中，作者通过之前的分析提到人们虽然愿意选择有机农业的作物作为食物来源，但因其产量不足以满足全球所有人的需求，有机农业还有很长的路要走(**Therefore**, there is still a long way to find a suitable solution that...)。

(三)课例展示

教材：新剑桥第三册第四单元文本 *Will Computers Ever Be More Intelligent than People*?

文本分析：本文中，作者以电脑是否能比人类更加聪明为话题，通过分析电脑的优势和人具有的优势，最后得出自己的观点。在信息时代，电脑和人工智能的作用越来越明显，这是一个很值得深思的话题,究竟谁能主宰未来? 作者的观点可以作为阅读的起点,诱发学生进行更深层的思考,为未来的生活、科技、教育等方面提供先见性预设。

教学目标

1. 厘清文章结构及论证手段;
2. 针对电脑是否能比人类更智能等未来生活预测系列问题进行思考和讨论。

教学步骤

Activity 1: Lead-in

你知道 AlphaGo 和李世石的比赛吗?

Activity 2: Reading

再读一遍文章,回答以下问题。

Which paragraph:

1) develops one side of the argumentation?

2) gives the opposing argumentation?

3) sums up the writer's main ideas?

4) says what the writer is writing about?

你知道议论文的基本结构吗?

—Introduction

—Discussion/Argument

—Conclusion

Activity 3: Discussion

按照议论文的结构,选择一个写作主题。

Will There Still Be Schools and Teachers in the Future?

Will It Be Possible to Live Forever?

Will E-books Take the Place of Traditional Books?

Will Human Cloning Be Widely Used?

Activity 4: Homework

按照议论文的结构写一篇作文。

(四)技巧归纳

通过分析,此类议论文所运用的技巧如下:

1) 论点、论据布局清晰。两种行文结构,作者无论是先表明观点,再具体分点论述,还是先分析现象，最后陈述观点，在文章结构上，作者的观点位置均清晰可见，论据素材均构成文章主体部分。

2）运用主旨句。主旨句使文章每一段的内容清晰而有层次，便于内容、思想的清晰传达，有利于读者迅速把握文章的整体脉络。

3）基于论据进行肯定或反驳，做到论证有基础。比如在 *Will Computers Ever Be More Intelligent than People*？一文中，作者先是肯定计算机作为伟大发明之一，功能强大，这也是其被认为会超越人脑的依据，而后第三段直接指出与人脑相比，计算机缺乏情感互动能力，直接推翻观点存续的基础，从而有力证明作者自己的观点，即计算机不会超越人脑。

4）句型参考：

This is a fascinating idea, but I don't believe...

Opinions vary from person to person/are divided as to this topic.

Let's explore several examples before coming to a reasonable conclusion.

Perhaps there is an element of truth in both these pictures. Personally, I hold that...

Based on what has been analyzed above, we may arrive at the conclusion that...

（五）迁移创新

仿写此类议论文，可以选取社会热点话题或现象作为迁移练习，如下面的话题：

随着钉钉、慕课、网络教学资源的丰富，学生似乎可以在教室之外享受丰富的课堂资源，那么学校和教师未来会被取代吗？请以 *Will There Still Be Schools and Teachers in the Future*？为题写一篇文章，阐述你的观点。

（六）作品舞台

学生作品 1

Nowadays, with the rapid development of technology and also due to the epidemic, online teaching or learning is seemingly becoming part of our life. Seeing the convenience of learning brought by the Internet, some people can't help asking whether there will be schools and teachers in the future. In my eyes, I don't think schools and teachers will disappear or be replaced in the future.

It is true that students can learn the knowledge more conveniently. Especially when they meet with difficult problems, they can search on the Internet for relative information. And various types of online class softwares, which make online learning convenient, are emerging constantly. This leads some people, who think students can learn almost everything online, to doubt the necessity of schools and teachers in the future.

However, the nature of education is more than the acquisition of knowledge. It is also about the interaction and communication between students and teachers in a face-to-face manner. The humanistic feelings in the process cannot be transmitted through networks. Schools are actually the best place for students to experience the charm of education, to develop the social-emotional ability and make preparations for the future life. All the above are irreplaceable.

So although the Internet or online teaching provides a platform for teachers' teaching and students' learning and facilitates education largely, I still believe that schools and teachers will not be replaced in the future.

教师点评：

作者从现状出发，首段首先表明自己观点，认为学校和教师在未来会依旧存在。而后第二段从正面肯定了这个问题存在的合理性，即不少人对教师和学校在未来存在的必要性提出疑问是基于现在网络的发展和网课的便利。第三段从教育的本质出发，论述学校和教师的功能在情感交互、沟通交流等方面是无法替代的，同时这也是网课所不具备的，从而有力支撑自己的观点。这篇作文很好地借鉴了教材课文的结构和论证方式，即先承认其合理性，而后从反面证明其局限性，很好地做到了学以致用。

学生作品 2

Will there still be schools and teachers in the future? Well, we need a little analysis before arriving at the conclusion.

To start with, let's review the different forms of schools throughout history. In ancient times, young people and kids went to schools which were referred to as "xuetang". The teachers were called "fuzi". At that time, they did not have modern conveniences like projectors and digital blackboards. But now we almost have classes in a similar way. So, in the future, I guess people will still have classes in classrooms. But maybe the schools are virtual or something like that. But schools will exist.

Secondly, considering the poor concentration and lack of self-discipline among teenagers and young people, I am convinced that teachers will be around in the future. Parents do contribute to the teaching of children, but the future society will feature high efficiency and student affairs are still in the control of the teachers.

To sum up, schools and teachers may vary in their way of work, but the roles they play are irreplaceable. So, I'd say yes.

教师点评：

本文作者以一种叙述的口吻来展开问题的分析：先从学校和教师的古今对比入手，指出学校的存在是历史的必然，在将来也是不可替代的；接着以对青少年和年轻人缺乏自律和专注力的分析，指出学习的监督工作虽然可以由家长负责，但在高度高效的将来，教学的事情主要还是依靠教师来负责；最后，作者自然地得出了自己的结论。

五、提出—分析—解决问题类

(一)类别解析

该类问题常常是针对社会上或生活中存在的某个问题提出解决方法,常见结构模式为开篇提出问题、而后分析问题产生的原因或者危害、最后提出问题的解决办法。提出问题、分析问题、解决问题,整个过程也是作者形成并最终表明自己观点或提出解决方案的过程。

(二)精研文本

以人教版新教材必修第一册第二单元 Workbook 中的课文 *Be a Good Tourist* 为例进行分析。

文章首段引入话题,提出问题:旅游业的发展有利有弊,既可以促进经济发展、增加就业,但同时游客本身又会引发一些问题。第二段具体阐述问题一:游客在旅游胜地乱涂乱刻,破坏了旅游胜地的人文建筑等,并针对该问题提出自己的观点和建议,即停下来,用友善和爱去影响他人,从而在世界上留下自己的痕迹。第三段具体阐述问题二:游客打扰当地人的生活,并具体举例说明,而后提出自己的观点和建议,即成为一个思虑周到、体贴的人,用不打扰他人的方式进行旅游。第四段是总述,再次排比罗列问题,证明游客带来问题之多的同时,进一步提出自己的建议,即解决此类问题的根本在于从自我做起,确保自己不是其中之一。除了首段是引入话题外,其余三段每一段都呼应文章标题,明确具体地阐释了 how to be a good tourist。

再如人教版新教材必修第二册第一单元中的 *From Problems to Solutions* 这篇文章。乍一看,这篇文章的文体不是特别典型,但仔细分析之后会发现它是以阿斯旺大坝的具体例子来说明国际合作是解决一些重大问题的有力途径。文章一开始提到了在进步和文化古迹保护之间取得平衡是很困难的事情,接着具体提出了阿斯旺大坝的修建威胁到当地文化古迹的问题,然后以埃及政府解决这两者矛盾的过程为主题,描述了 establish a committee、investigate the issue、make a proposal、sign a document、take down the cultural sites piece by piece、put together 等过程,历时 20 年,在 50 多个国家的帮助下,成功将神庙迁移到安全的地方。作者接着提出:"… it was possible for countries to work together to build a better tomorrow."最后一段的总结中,作者提到:"The spirit of the Aswan Dam project is still alive today… If a problem seems too difficult for a single nation, the global community can sometimes provide a solution."这种通过具体事例来说理的方式显得具有情境性,读者被带到故事的背景中,深深地参与其中,说理也水到渠成。

（三）课例展示

教材：人教版新教材必修第二册第一单元文本 *From Problems to Solutions*

文本分析：*From Problems to Solutions* 这篇文章讲述了阿斯旺大坝在修建过程中所遇到的问题，以及最后通过国际合作的方式得以解决。本文的话题是文化遗产与社会经济发展的冲突，以及所面临的挑战，旨在让学生分析探讨问题的解决，认识到文化遗产保护需要世界各国和全社会共同努力，并进一步思考自己在生活中如何切实参与到文化遗产保护的行动中。

文本内容有深远的文化意义，有助于培养思维品质。文本结构清晰，按照时间顺序记述事件发展过程，第一段为问题的提出（general problem），第二段分析问题（concrete problem—Aswan Dam），第三、四段解决问题（committee，funds，experts，environmentalists—how to do），第五、六段为问题解决的结果及意义（result and significance）。每个段落的结构清晰，主题句明晰，例证恰当，可以让学生更清楚地理解文本。本课时以 problem 和 solution 为主线，以 Aswan Dam 为例让学生整体理解文本。

教学目标

1. 根据标题和图片预测文章内容，运用略读策略，找出各段的主题句和段落大意，制作时间线，培养学生的逻辑思维能力；

2. 通过自主阅读，勾画文本框架结构，找出面临的 problem 和 solution，思考"Should the old give way to the new?"锻炼学生的批判性思维；

3. 通过合作探究解决问题的方法，思考自己在生活中如何参与到文化遗产保护的行动中，培养学生的创新性思维。

教学步骤

Activity 1：Lead-in & predict

激活已知，带入情境。

Today we will go to Egypt，what do you know about it?

Pictures offered：pyramids，the Sphinx，Abu Simbel Temple，the Aswan Dam…

Read the title and look at the photos. What do you think the text is about?

Activity 2：Getting the main idea

运用略读策略，获取文章主旨大意，了解如何判定文中的关键信息和主题句；通过分析文体结构，帮助学生找出解决办法，引导学生积极主动解决问题。

1）Check your guessing and find out the "problem" and "solution".

2）Identity the structure of the text.

3）Find out the topic sentence and functional sentences.

Activity 3：Getting the detailed information

对于基于时间顺序叙述的文章，教师可引导学生用时间线来梳理事件，对比修建大坝的利弊，锻炼学生的批判性思维，引导学生探索解决问题的方法。

1）Circle the numbers in the text and understand what they mean.

2）Complete the timeline with the information in the text.

3）Advantages and disadvantages of building a new dam.

4）Sort out UN's specific ways to solve the problem with a mind map. Guess how the temples and other cultural sites were saved.（视频资料）

5）What words can you think of to describe the project?

Activity 4：Discussion

通过任务的实施，让学生把所学应用到实际活动中。

1）Interview：Taking economic development into consideration，what can you do to protect our cultural heritage?

2）Discussion：A lot of money was spent to protect the temples. Do you think it was worthwhile? Why or why not?

3）Why do you think so many countries contributed funds and offered help to the Egyptian project?

4）Why is it important to protect and preserve our cultural heritage?

Activity 5：Homework（二选一）

1）某中学生英文报就保护中国传统文化为主题举行英语征文活动，你准备给该报投稿，稿件内容包括：

①保护中国传统文化的重要性；

②列举 1~2 个你所知道的国家或当地政府文化保护的事例；

③谈谈你对文化保护的建议。

2）自选话题，将本文借助具体事例来说理的写作方法用于写作中，写一篇 100 词左右的议论文。

（四）技巧归纳

通过分析，此类议论文所运用的技巧如下：

1）有观点论述，有实例支撑。观点类表述如：第二段指出重大的挑战有时会引出伟大的解决措施，接下来就详细说明了阿斯旺大坝建设中遇到的挑战及解决方法；

2）紧扣话题，通过中心句和事例的叙述将论点具体化，通过文末的讨论对主题进行升华。

3）句型参考：

问题陈述部分：

Recently/Nowadays, ... has become a serious problem we have to face.

The phenomenon... has aroused the public's concern.

分析（原因/后果）：

There are several reasons accounting for the problem.

A variety of factors contribute to the phenomenon.

问题解决：

People have figured out many ways to solve the problem.

It is high time that we figured out ways to deal with the problem.

With joint efforts, I am confident that...

（五）迁移创新

此类练习，可结合学生的网课和线下课堂的实际，从身边生活感悟入手，如：学生群体中也有适应当下形势者，他们的学习并没有受到学习条件变化的影响。如何在线上和线下的课堂中做一个合格的学习者呢？请以 *Be a Qualified Learner in Online/Offline Classes* 为题来完成一篇写作。

（六）作品舞台

学生作品 1

In the past three years, we have ushered in the era of online classes, which bring much convenience and also expose many problems. After a period of online courses, there are many once excellent students whose learning has plummeted. Meanwhile, many dark horses have emerged. This issue is worth thinking.

The first problem is idleness. An old saying goes, "Sloth sharpens the edge of the wisdom". Always some students use the excuses such as "oversleep for five more minutes" "finish the homework right away" to deceive themselves. And before they know it, time has passed and the gap between them and others has widened step by step. In my eyes, the best way to avoid this happening is to make a to-do list or a timetable. Be goal-oriented and work to achieve given goals to overcome the sloth or procrastination.

Another big problem is the unreasonable use of electronics. When we have online classes, there are usually other electronic devices next to us, which will distract our attention so that we cannot concentrate on our classes. For instance, play with mobile phones late at night and don't get up in time in the morning, forming a vicious circle. The solution to the problem is to seek the supervision of family members or classmates and learn to be self-disciplined, such as setting an alarm clock to strictly control the time spent on playing electronics.

Any problems can be overcome with a willing heart. Be self-disciplined, act effectively and fight against sloth to be a qualified online learner.

教师点评:

作者开篇首先指出,网课时代的到来有利有弊,网课期间陨落一片星辰,也会冲出一群黑马,接着从问题出发,进行具体举例分析,而后提出解决方案,最后一段进行总结重申:只有自律、勤奋、切实行动才能成为一个合格的网络学习者。作者仿照教材行文结构,整体结构清晰,从发现问题到分析问题,再到最后提出解决方案,且方案内容较为具体,切实可行。

学生作品2

After the end of the online classes, we return to the long-lost campus, with everything back to normal. But we may find ourselves out of tune with the fast pace of offline classes. Then how should we adapt ourselves to be qualified learners in offline classes?

Take my classmate Li Ming as an example. During the pandemic, he kept a strict timetable set by himself, getting up at 6 o'clock in the morning, taking online courses and doing a daily review and summary. A lot of students abandoned themselves to entertainment or depression, while Li Ming remained positive. When we return to school, life seems as usual for Li Ming. He applies himself to class discussions, autonomous learning and project research. As for him, classes are a platform for him. The stage may vary, but the core remains the same: to improve, to concentrate and to strive for the dream of becoming a scientist in his heart.

Young people nowadays are constantly faced with numerous lures. The lesson of Li Ming reminds us of the importance of self-disciple, long-term goals and a positive mind in the face of difficulties.

教师点评:

本文作者从自己同学李明的例子出发展开论证,揭示学习中的自我约束、长期目标和乐观态度的重要性,结合普通人的生动故事的说理显得并不枯燥。在平时的口笔头表达中,学生往往对鸿篇巨制的大作文有畏难情绪,短小而生活化的小短文是实现这种过渡的必要过程。

第五节　读后续写

（一）类别解析

读后续写是高考英语改革即一年两考增加的新题型，替代短文改错题型。该题型初现于2016年浙江省高考英语试卷中，并随着高考改革试点的扩大逐渐应用在全国各地。“读”的短文词数在350词左右，通俗易懂、故事性较强。文章体裁以记叙文或夹叙夹议文为主，语篇主题涵盖人与自然、人与社会、人与自我。

浙江省在2016年第一次使用新题型“读后续写”，之后在全国高考试题中被广泛应用。《普通高等学校招生全国统一考试英语学科考试说明》（高考综合改革试验省份试用）（第一版）对读后续写题型提出了明确的要求：

提供一段350词以内的语言材料，要求考生根据材料内容、所给段落开头语和所标示关键词进行续写（150词左右），将其发展成一篇与给定材料有逻辑衔接、情节和结构完整的短文。

A. 样题

第二节：读后续写（满分25分）

阅读下面短文，根据所给情节进行续写，使之构成一个完整的故事。

A funny thing happened to Arthur when he was on the way to work one day. As he walked along Park Avenue near the First National Bank, he heard the sound of someone trying to start a car. He tried again and again but couldn't get the car moving. Arthur turned and looked inside at the face of a young man who looked worried. Arthur stopped and asked, "It looks like you've got a problem," Arthur said.

"I'm afraid so. I'm in a big hurry and I can't start my car."

"Is there something I can do to help?" Arthur asked. The young man looked at the two suitcases in the back seat and then said, "Thanks. If you're sure it wouldn't be too much trouble, you could help me get these suitcases into a taxi."

"No trouble at all. I'd be glad to help."

The young man got out and took one of the suitcases from the back seat. After placing it on the ground, he turned to get the other one. Just as Arthur picked up the first suitcase and started walking, he heard the long loud noise of an alarm.

It was from the bank. There had been a robbery!

Park Avenue had been quiet a moment before. Now the air was filled with the sound of the alarm and the shouts of people running from all directions. Cars stopped and the passengers joined the crowd in front of the bank. People asked each other, "What happened?" But everyone had a different answer.

Arthur, still carrying the suitcase, turned to look at the bank and walked right into the young woman in front of him.

She looked at the suitcase and then at him. Arthur was surprised. "Why is she looking at me like that?" He thought. "The suitcase! She thinks I'm the bank thief!"

Arthur looked around at the crowd of people. He became frightened, and without another thought, he started to run.

注意：

1. 所续写短文的词数应为 150 词左右；
2. 应使用 5 个以上短文中标有下划线的关键词语；
3. 续写部分分为两段，每段的开头语已为你写好；
4. 续写完成后，请用下划线标出你所使用的关键词语。

Paragraph 1：

As he was running, Arthur heard the young man shouting behind, "Stop, stop!" ________

____

____

____

____

Paragraph 2：

The taxi stopped in front of the Police Station and Arthur ________

____

____

____

____

One possible version：

As he was running, Arthur heard the young man shouting behind, "Stop, stop!" Arthur immediately realized that the young man was the bank robber. So Arthur didn't stop, but continued to run until he saw and caught a taxi in front of him. He quickly put the suitcase into the car and said to the driver, "Please hurry to the Police Station. I have a case to report to the police. The man shouting behind is the bank thief!" The taxi raced away to the Police Station like an arrow.

The taxi stopped in front of the Police Station and Arthur said to the police who had been waiting and who had already received the robbery report, "This suitcase is that of the bank robber. It may be filled with the money stolen from the bank. I hand it to you. Please get ready to arrest the man."

B. 读后续写考查汇总

2016 年至 2024 年 1 月浙江卷、新高考Ⅰ卷和新高考Ⅱ卷都多次考查了读后续写。2016 年 10 月浙江省首次采用读后续写,之后浙江卷读后续写考查情况如下表,其中 2018 年 11 月和 2019 年 6 月采用概要写作。浙江省于 2023 年 6 月采用新高考Ⅰ卷。

时间	卷别	主题	词数	难度	故事主题
2024.1	浙江卷	人与自我	302+28	4.49	方向感差的 Eva 战胜自己
2023.6	新高考Ⅰ&Ⅱ卷	人与自我	318+24	4.01	在老师的鼓励下参加作文比赛
2023.1	浙江卷	人与自然	337+20	4.56	"我"与蜂鸟的神奇邂逅
2022.6	新高考Ⅰ&Ⅱ卷	人与自我	306+27	4.02	鼓励身残志坚的男孩继续参加越野赛
2022.6	浙江卷	人与社会	322+28	3.98	为无家可归的人们发放食物
2022.1	浙江卷	人与社会	331+25	4.94	与"最不合拍"搭档成为好友
2021.6	新高考Ⅰ &Ⅱ卷	人与自我	308+22	3.98	母亲节,双胞胎为母亲做早餐失败后爸爸帮忙
2021.6	浙江卷	人与自我	302+14	4.27	作者上学时的一次打工挣钱的经历
2021.1	浙江卷	人与社会	338+19	4.37	万圣节时少年意外将头卡在南瓜中而在网络上爆红
2020.7	浙江卷	人与自然	300+18	4.82	拍摄北极熊遇险
2020.7	新高考Ⅰ卷	人与社会	313+25	4	Meredith 通过制作和卖爆米花帮助邻居摆脱困境
2020.1	浙江卷	人与自然	336+20	3.86	男孩离家上大学,缺失玩伴的小狗也很沮丧
2018.6	浙江卷	人与自我	316+22	4.01	我和爸爸骑马游玩却在山里迷路

续表

时间	卷别	主题	词数	难度	故事主题
2017.11	浙江卷	人与自我	338+27	4	母亲总是健忘落下东西
2017.6	浙江卷	人与自然	341+16	4.39	狼口脱险
2016.10	浙江卷	人与自我	330+18	3.97	丈夫与妻子在森林露营遇险

C. 读后续写阅读文本难度及句法分析

对读后续写中阅读文章难度的评估采用在线工具——“英语阅读分级指难针”。该工具由华南师范大学开发，可从词汇、句法与文本三个维度提供难度评估。以 2021 年 1 月浙江卷为例，难度指标报告显示如下：

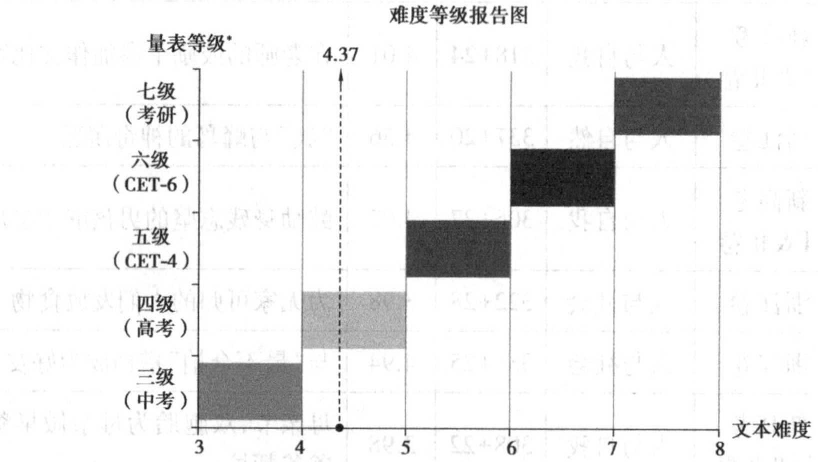

*参照《中国英语能力等级量表》（2018）

难度指标报告表

类别	量化指标	对应等级
词汇难度	4.87	四级（高考）
句法难度	4.27	四级（高考）
文本难度	4.37	四级（高考）

阅读分级指难针

句法分析

◉限定性从属子句	○复杂名词短语	○非限定性动词短语
11	22	21

Pumpkin（南瓜）carving at Halloween is a family tradition. We visit a local farm every October. In the pumpkin field, I compete with my three brothers and sister to seek out the biggest pumpkin. My dad has a rule that we **have** to carry our pumpkins back home, and **as** the eldest child I **have** an advantage—I **carried** an 85-pounder back last year.

This year, it was hard to tell whether my prize or the one chosen by my 14-year-old brother, Jason, **was** the winner. Unfortunately we forgot to weigh them before taking out their insides, but I was determined to prove my point. All of us were hard at work at the kitchen table, with my mom filming the annual event. I'm unsure now why I **thought** forcing my head inside the pumpkin would settle the matter, but it seemed to make perfect sense at the time.

With the pumpkin resting on the table, hole uppermost, I bent over and pressed my head against the opening. At first I got jammed just above my eyes and then, **as I went** on with my task, unwilling to quit, my nose briefly prevented entry. Finally I managed to put my whole head into it, like a cork（软木塞）forced into a bottle. I was able to straighten up with the huge pumpkin resting on my shoulders.

My excitement was short-lived. The pumpkin was heavy. "I'm going to set it down, now," I said, and with Jason helping to support its weight, I bent back over the table to give it somewhere to rest. It was only when I **tried** to remove my head that I **realized** getting out **was** going to be less straightforward than getting in. When I **pulled** hard, my nose got in the way. I got into a panic as I **pressed** firmly against the table and **moved** my head around trying to find the right angle, but it was no use. "I can't get it out!" I shouted, my voice sounding unnaturally loud in the enclosed space.

（本文共计 340 词，最长句子 30 词）

注：

1）"限定性从属子句"包括定语从句、状语从句和名词性从句等；"复杂名词短语"包括由形容词、所有格、介词短语、定语从句、现在分词或过去分词等修饰的名词短语；"非限定性动词短语"包括动词不定式、动名词短语和过去分词短语等；

2）工具已对子句或短语中的核心单词进行标注、提供结构提示，用户可根据提示划分完整的子句或短语；

3）工具已使用下划线对文本中的最长句子进行标注；

4）分析结果可能存在少量误差。

阅读分级指难针

词汇分析

○中考阶段　◉高考阶段　○CET-4 阶段　○CET-6 阶段　○考研阶段

91.12%　96.45%　96.45%　99.41%　99.41%

Pumpkin（南瓜）carving at Halloween is a family tradition. We visit a local farm every October. In the **pumpkin** field, I compete with my three brothers and sister to seek out the biggest **pumpkin**. My dad has a rule that we have to carry our **pumpkins** back home, and as the **eldest** child I have an advantage—I carried an 85-**pounder** back last year.

This year, it was hard to tell whether my prize or the one chosen by my 14-year-old brother, Jason, was the winner. Unfortunately we forgot to weigh them before taking out their insides, but I was determined to prove my point. All of us were hard at work at the kitchen table, with my mom filming the annual event. I'm unsure now why I thought forcing my head inside the **pumpkin** would settle the matter, but it seemed to make perfect sense at the time.

With the **pumpkin** resting on the table, hole uppermost, I bent over and pressed my head against the opening. At first I got jammed just above my eyes and then, as I went on with my task, unwilling to quit, my nose briefly prevented entry. Finally I managed to put my whole head into it, like a **cork**（软木塞）forced into a bottle. I was able to straighten up with the huge **pumpkin** resting on my shoulders.

My excitement was short-lived. The **pumpkin** was heavy. "I'm going to set it down, now," I said, and with Jason helping to support its weight, I bent back over the table to give it somewhere to rest. It was only when I tried to remove my head that I realized getting out was going to be less straightforward than getting in. When I pulled hard, my nose got in the way. I got into a panic as I pressed firmly against the table and moved my head around trying to find the right angle, but it was no use. "I can't get it out!" I shouted, my voice sounding unnaturally loud in the **enclosed** space.

阅读难度及句法分析：

语篇	难度系数	限定性从属子句	复杂名词短语	非限定性动词短语	最长句子词数
2024.1 浙江卷	4.49	12	22	16	21
2023.6 新高考Ⅰ & Ⅱ卷	4.01	14	16	14	35
2023.1 浙江卷	4.56	10	23	12	22

续表

语篇	难度系数	限定性从属子句	复杂名词短语	非限定性动词短语	最长句子词数
2022.6 新高考Ⅰ&Ⅱ卷	4.02	18	26	8	32
2022.6 浙江卷	3.98	16	22	22	30
2022.1 浙江卷	4.94	23	18	14	36
2021.6 新高考Ⅰ&Ⅱ卷	3.98	10	20	9	22
2021.6 浙江卷	4.27	15	27	7	34
2021.1 浙江卷	4.37	11	22	21	30
2020.7 浙江卷	4.82	11	29	8	23
2020.7 新高考Ⅰ卷	4	14	21	9	25
2020.1 浙江卷	3.86	9	28	11	29
2018.6 浙江卷	4.01	4	17	12	29
2017.11 浙江卷	4	19	24	5	43
2017.6 浙江卷	4.39	8	25	9	27
2017.6 浙江卷	3.97	12	20	15	23

“指难针”对以上术语界定如下：“限定性从属子句”包括定语从句、状语从句和名词性从句等；“复杂名词短语”包括由形容词、所有格、介词短语、定语从句、现在分词或过去分词等修饰的名词短语；“非限定性动词短语”包括动词不定式、动名词短语和过去分词短语等。

以 2022 年新高考Ⅰ卷为例，读后续写阅读文本的难度为 4.02，难度略低于阅读理解 B 篇(4.19)、C 篇(4.21)、D 篇(4.88)(李芷莹，金檀，2022)。其中，“指难针”所检测的句法分析与人工检测关联程度为 100%，分析准确，可为读后续写命题文本提供可靠依据。

鉴于以上分析，新高考Ⅰ&Ⅱ卷的读后续写文本难度较为稳定，难度系数范围为 3.98~4.02，且难度略低于浙江卷。浙江卷难度系数范围为 3.86~4.94，波动较大。个别年份阅读文本的难度超过阅读理解的 C 篇和 D 篇。

此外，阅读文本的难度系数和限定性从属子句个数、非限定性动词短语基本呈正相关。鉴于此，教师在日常教学中应强化学生的语法运用能力和长难句分析能力。

D. 语篇主题分析

在读后续写文章的语篇主题中,“人与自我”主题考查得最多,占 46%;“人与社会”“人与自然”主题均占比 27%。其中,“人与自我”话题涵盖了生活与学习、做人和做事子主题群,尤其主题语境内容包含个人,家庭、社区及学校生活,正确的人生态度,公民义务与社会责任。

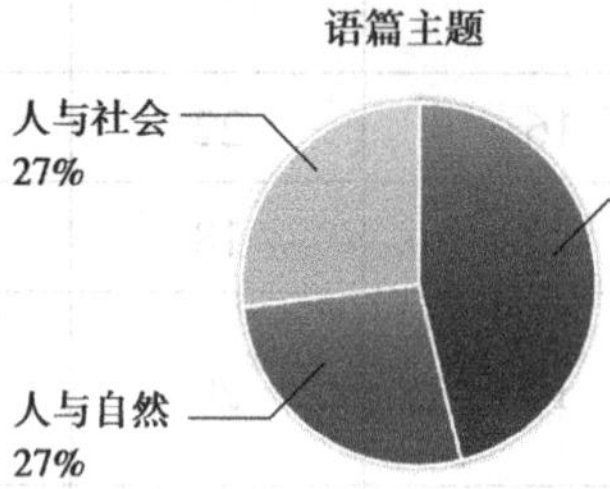

(二)精研文本

对读写结合教学实践,广大教师关注已久,但是,写作多涉及文学作品读后感、改写原文本故事情节及结局,读后总结、与主题相关的应用文写作等。其中,改写故事与读后续写均属于创造性写作,基于文本又超越原文本。人教版新教材中的部分记叙文可以进行读后续写设计。

A. 读后续写文本分析案例

人教版新教材为读后续写提供了案例,执教者可以改编原文,使之与读后续写考查一致。

册次	板块	题目
必修第二册 Unit 4	Reading for Writing	Beautiful Ireland and Its Traditions
必修第三册 Unit 1	Reading for Writing	My Amazing Naadam Experience
必修第三册 Unit 2	Reading for Writing	The Stone in the Road
必修第三册 Unit 2 (Workbook)	Reading and Writing	The Taxi Ride I'll Never Forget
必修第三册 Unit 5 (Workbook)	Expanding Your World	My Uncle Jules (Adapted)
选择性必修第四册 Unit 1	Reading and Thinking	Satisfaction Guaranteed (Adapted)

B. 文本分析方式

“怎么读”和“读什么”是师生面对读后续写文本时面临的主要问题。在理解文章主旨大意和段落大意的基础上,可以借助如下方法,厘清文本主要信息,为续写奠定基础。

☆ "5W+1H"六要素分析法

对记叙文的分析,主要采用"5W+1H"六要素分析法,即 when, where, who, what, why 和 how。其中,时间(when)和地点(where)明晰了故事背景(setting),who 指人物(character),what 指主要情节(plot),why 指故事的主题(theme),也可以指故事意图(intention);而 how 指结局(result)、情感(feeling)或冲突(conflicts)。

下面以人教版新教材必修第三册第二单元课文 *The Taxi Ride I'll Never Forget* 为例,讲解如何通过对文本进行分析厘清文章主要内容,快速获得信息。

The Taxi Ride I'll Never Forget

When	At midnight
Where	On the way to a hospice
What	The old lady asked the driver to drive through the city to recall her life
Who	The old lady and I
Why	To cherish the small precious moments of life and value what we have
How	The old lady: sad, lonely, grateful I (the taxi driver): sympathetic, satisfied

虽然"5W+1H"六要素分析法能快速厘清文本的基本信息,但若文本中涉及人物(character/role)较多,该分析方式就会存在明显不足。此外,这一分析方式不能很好地反映语篇中人物的内心活动以及人物之间的冲突,这时就可以采用其他分析方式。

☆ Action-Response-Emotion(ARE)方法

文本内容的分析主要分为两步,即解释(explain)内容和丰富(enrich)内容。解释内容主要为文本走向、背景分析等;丰富内容则主要从 action、response、emotion 等角度进行。

Action-Response-Emotion 聚焦文本中人物的动作、反应、情绪,从而反映人物内心的冲突、微表情和微动作。采用这一方式对人教版新教材选择性必修第三册第二单元 Reading for Writing 的文本 *The Stone in the Road* 进行分析如下。

Characters	Actions	Responses	Emotions
Milkman	crashed into the stone	went away	angry, indifferent
Woman with water	tripped over the stone	picked herself up and limped away in tears	sad, fragile

Continued

Characters	Actions	Responses	Emotions
Other villagers	complained about the stone	nobody made an attempt to move the stone	unhappy, selfish
Young girl	succeed in moving the stone to the side of the street	—	responsible, considerate…

以 2021 年 6 月浙江卷高考读后续写文本分析如下：

My dad, George, only had an eighth grade education. A quiet man, he didn't understand my world of school activities. From age 14, he worked. And his dad, Albert, took the money my dad earned and used it to pay family expenses.

I didn't really understand his world either: He was a livestock trucker, and I thought that I would surpass（超过）anything he had accomplished by the time I walked across the stage at high school graduation.

Summers in the mid-70s were spent at home shooting baskets, hitting a baseball, or throwing a football, preparing for my future as a quarterback on a football team. In poor weather, I read about sports or practiced my trombone（长号）.

The summer before my eighth grade I was one of a group of boys that a neighboring farmer hired to work in his field. He explained our basic task, the tractor fired up and we were off, riding down the field looking for weeds to spray with chemicals. After a short way, the farmer stopped and pointed at a weed which we missed. Then we began again. This happened over and over, but we soon learned to identify different grasses like cockleburs, lamb's quarters, footails, and the king of weeds, the pretty purple thistle. It was tiring work, but I looked forward to the pay, even though I wasn't sure how much it would amount to.

At home, my dad said, "A job's a big step to growing up. I'm glad you will be contributing to the household." My dad's words made me realize that my earnings might not be mine to do with as I wished.

My labors lasted about two weeks, and the farmer said there might be more work, but I wasn't interested. I decided it was not fair that I had to contribute my money.

Paragraph 1: The pay arrived at last.

____

Paragraph 2: I understood immediately what my parents were worried about.

____

Characters	Actions	Responses	Emotions
Grandpa	took my father's wage, paid for family expenses	—	—
Dad	supported, worked	contributed to the family	willing, glad
I	worked during the summer vacation; didn't want to contribute	was not interested in more work	not willing, unfair

这种分析方法也可以运用到写作中，丰富文章的内容。第一段中应提到获得劳动报酬之后，小男孩和父亲的反应和情绪，以及对应的动作有哪些，以此来丰富写作的内容。教师可以设置问题链，帮助学生打开思路。如：1) How did I feel upon receiving the pay? 2) How did my parents react when seeing my reaction? 第二段提到"我"明白了父亲的担忧，可针对 action 和 response 设置问题链，如：1) What did my parents say or do then? 2) How did I feel when learning the truth? 3) What did I learn from it?

☆ Story Mountain"故事山"分析法

Story Mountain（故事山）是梳理文本情节的有效视觉辅助工具之一。从 Story Mountain 的一侧出发，到达故事的高潮，再沿 Story Mountain 的另一侧走向故事结尾。Story Mountain 一般由 Introduction—Rising Action—Climax—Falling Action—Resolution—Ending 这几个环节构成。

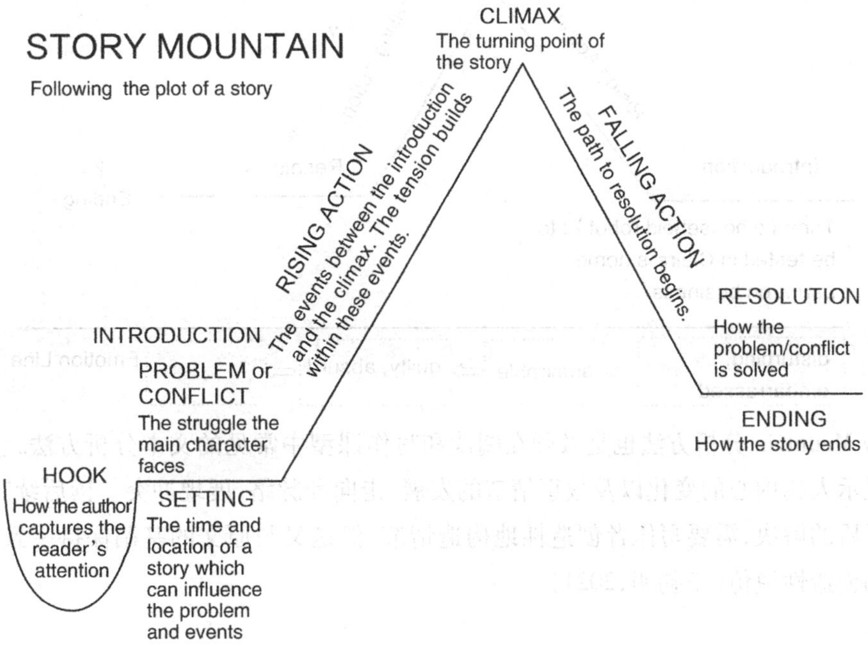
STORY MOUNTAIN
Following the plot of a story
CLIMAX
The turning point of the story
RISING ACTION
The events between the introduction and the climax. The tension builds within these events.
FALLING ACTION
The path to resolution begins.
INTRODUCTION
PROBLEM or CONFLICT
The struggle the main character faces
HOOK
How the author captures the reader's attention
SETTING
The time and location of a story which can influence the problem and events
RESOLUTION
How the problem/conflict is solved
ENDING
How the story ends

Introduction 是指在正式进入 Story Mountain 之前,先介绍故事发生的时间、地点、背景等基本要素,具体划分为 Hook—Problem/Conflict—Setting,将读者引入故事。

Rising Action 在 Introduction 之后,正式开始 Story Mountain 的旅程。每个故事都有矛盾和冲突,在 Rising Action 部分,作者会详细描述角色遇到的困境和需要完成的事情,为故事高潮的到来蓄势。

Climax:随着故事情节的发展,读者逐渐攀登 Story Mountain,直到到达山顶,也就是故事的高潮部分。这里会抛出故事角色面临的最大挑战,内容常常扣人心弦,充斥着各种各样的情感、闹剧和悬念。

Falling Action:经历过紧张刺激的 Climax 部分,读者从 Story Mountain 的顶点离开,走向下山的路。这段路程中也会有一些事情发生,但是故事发展的进程会变慢。

Resolution:随着故事的推进,高潮中展现的冲突得以解决。

Ending:故事降下帷幕。

读后续写中的阅读文本一般包含 Introduction、Rising Action、Climax 部分,Falling Action、Resolution 和 Ending 部分多为续写内容,要求读者在原文基础上进行再创造。运用这一策略分析时,学生还可以增加 Emotion Line,以表现故事人物情感态度的变化。以选择性必修第四册 Reading and Thinking 的文本 *Satisfaction Guaranteed* 为基础分析如下:

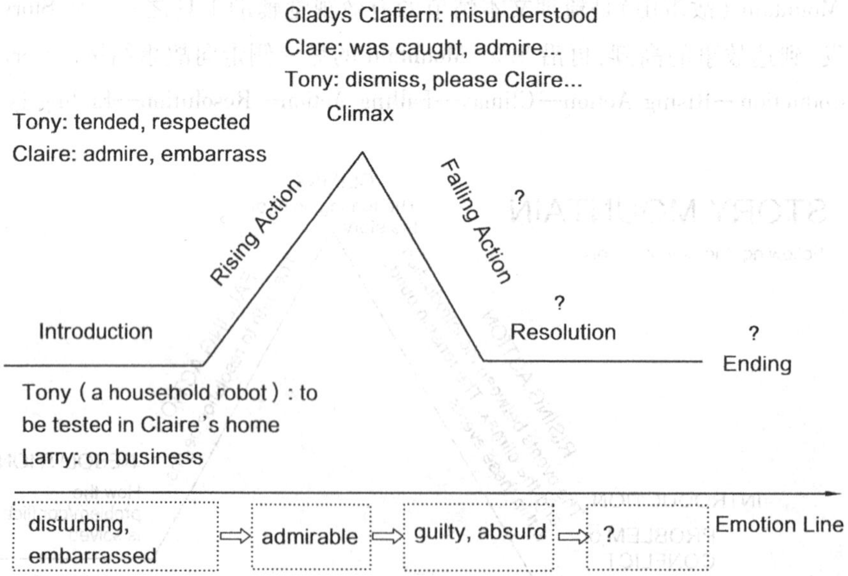

Story Mountain 分析方法也是教师在阅读和写作课型中常见的文本分析方法,它能清晰有效地展示人物内心的变化以及故事情节的发展、走向和脉络,展现冲突。读后续写聚焦于冲突与矛盾的解决,需要写作者创造性地构造情节,但是又与原文的基调保持一致,即与原文协同的创造性模仿(王初明,2021)。

☆**拉波夫叙事模式**

拉波夫(W. Labov)主张把语言放到社会中去研究,他的叙事分析模式在西方叙事学中有着重要的影响。这一分析模式来源于对个人口头叙事材料的研究,认为一个完整的叙事结构应包含以下六个部分:点题(Abstract)、指向(Orientation)、进展(Complication)、评议(Evaluation)、结局(Resolution)和回应(Coda)。实际应用中,有些语篇不具备完整的六要素,尤其结局和回应常常会重合。

拉波夫叙事模式概述		读后续写对应
点题	叙事时对故事的简要概述,一般用于故事开头,可指向故事的主题	记叙文六要素(5W+1H)
指向	叙事的时间、地点、人物、环境描述,为事件开展做铺垫	
进展	故事发展变化的描述,按照一定的顺序,通过人物语言、动作、心理描写等来呈现故事的曲折性	故事进展与冲突
评议	人物对事件的观点、态度,主要出现在进展和结局之间	人生观、价值观的形成,学科育人
结局	故事人物和事件的最终结果的交代	故事结局与主题升华
回应	故事与现实的链接、故事对现实的影响和赋予现实生活的意义,通常表达作者的感悟和价值取向,升华故事主题	

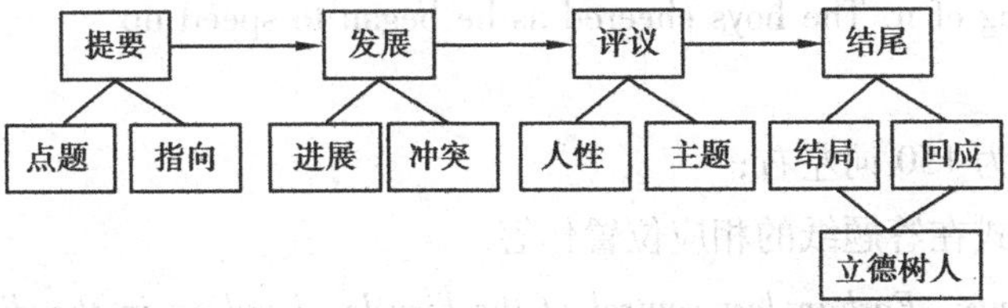

拉波夫叙事模式在高中英语读后续写中的建构和应用(崔文华,唐书哲,2023)

如果读后续写文本在矛盾与冲突的前提下,突出个人感悟或者人生观、价值观的形成,则适合使用拉波夫叙事模式进行分析。

下面以 2022 年嘉兴高三卷读后续写为例进行分析。

It wasn't fair.

Aminah always studied hard, so there was nothing unusual about her receiving top marks at the end of the year. But Farhan was often playing with the village boys when he should have been studying. To help motivate him this year, their father had promised to buy him a bicycle if his grades improved.

Aminah was sure that even this generous offer wouldn't change her brother's habits. But when Farhan started staying home and studying, everyone was surprised.

At the end of the school year, Aminah received top marks as she always did. And, as usual, her parents gave her 100 rupees (卢比) as a reward.

For the first time, Farhan got top marks too. True to his word, their father came home with a bicycle. It was well used, and much of the paint had been chipped (脱落) off. But to Farhan, it was the most beautiful bicycle in their country. Farhan's friends cheered when they saw it. It was understood that something as precious as a bicycle would be shared with everyone.

Well, almost everyone.

After a few days of watching Farhan and the village boys learning to ride, Aminah and her friends grew bitter. They spent afternoons on the hill just north of the village, sitting in the shade of a mango tree and watching the lazy stream flow at the foot of the hill. They could hear the boys cheering and laughing on the other side of the hill.

"Why doesn't he let us ride, Aminah?" asked Fatima. Aminah shrugged, trying to act as if she didn't care.

"He and the other boys just want the bicycle all for themselves!" replied Shehnaz. Sarah shook her head. "But Aminah is his sister! He should share with her." An older sister commanded respect.

As they talked, the boys' screams grew closer. Aminah looked up and saw her brother on his bicycle at the top of the hill. "Look! I can do it!" Farhan yelled at the top of his lungs. He had finally gotten the hang of it. The boys cheered as he began to speed up.

注意：

1. 续写词数应为150词左右；

2. 请按如下格式在答题纸的相应位置作答。

Para. 1: Suddenly, Farhan lost control of the bicycle, heading in the direction of the girls, toward the stream.

Para. 2: Farhan looked at Aminah, then at his bicycle, then back at his sister.

Abstract and Orientation	In a small village Aminah: studied hard, got top marks Her brother Farhan: played with the village boys, lack motivation in study Father: reward Farhan with a bicycle for his progress in study

Continued

Complication	Aminah grew bitter when seeing Farhan practice riding the bicycle; boys' cheers; Farhan sped up down a hill;...
Evaluation	Unfairness and envy between siblings
Resolution & Coda	(Open)

（三）课例展示

教材：新剑桥第三册第二单元 Speak and Read 板块中的文本 *Gelert—The Faithful Dog*

文本分析：本单元主题为 A True Friend，探讨人类朋友以及作为朋友的优秀品质，授课对象为高一学生。基于这个主题，本单元提供了四个文本。第一篇文本为记叙文，题目为 *Gelert—The Faithful Dog*，语篇主题为"人与自然"，故事背景设定于威尔士乡村，是故事的前半部分。第二篇文本为故事的后半部分和结局，全文由一个段落构成。第三篇文本为测试（Quiz），属于非连续性文本，通过完成 5 个题目来查看自己是否是忠诚的朋友（loyal friend）。第四篇文本为对话，主题为"人与社会"，讲述了 Laura 将采访歌手 Rapman 的机会让给朋友 Tom，因为 Tom 是该歌手的忠实粉丝，以此探讨朋友的意义和朋友之间的互帮互助。

本节课授课文本为第一篇，描述了主人公 Prince Llewllyn 外出狩猎，并让忠实的狗 Gelert 照看婴儿。狩猎途中，王子听到狗叫，深感不安，回家却发现婴儿不见了，而狗狗嘴角滴着血。王子误以为狗伤害了婴儿，怒而将其杀害。此文本共 171 字，第一段 64 字，第二段 107 字。通过指难针分析，文本总体难度为 3.64，其中词汇难度 3.74，句法难度为 3.34，约为中考难度。文本故事性强，注重细节描写和紧张氛围营造，尤其是动物的动作，如 gallop、blood drip、swung the sword、whimper 等。这些词汇超出了学生的认知，尤其是 drip、gallop、whim 为非考纲词汇，这也是本文词汇难度略高于文本难度的原因。读后续写课程中，读是写的基础，写是读的内化和迁移。有效的阅读输入是学习理解的第一步，接下来需要为在写作中丰富自己的语言提供帮助与支持。

总之，文本难度和语篇长度略低于读后续写高考题的文本难度，因此，较适合改为高一学生的读后续写素材。

本节课计划两个课时，教学设计如下：

教学目标)))

1. 理解故事情节，并欣赏文章描写动物动作的词汇（如 gallop、drip、whimper）和拟人修辞方法的使用；

2. 关注人与动物之间的信任，加深对狗的"忠诚"的理解；

3. 评价 Prince Llewllyn 杀死 Gelert 的行为，并小组讨论，预测狗被杀后故事的情节走向，续写故事；

4. 利用同伴、教师的分享和点评优化自身习作，提升自我评价和写作能力。

教学重难点)))

1. 厘清故事情节、故事发展及高潮，合理创设续写部分；（重点）

2. 分析 Gelert 的行为，并生动形象地描写狗的动作和 Prince Llewllyn 的心理活动。（难点）

教学过程)))

Activity 1：Lead-in

引入话题，激活背景知识。

教师呈现“狗”的图片，提问：“What do you know about dogs? Share your stories with dogs.”由于“狗”与人们的日常生活关系密切，有些学生甚至有养宠物狗的经历，所以该话题容易激起学生们讨论的兴趣。接着提问：“Do you think dogs are faithful friends? Illustrate your idea with examples.”学生思考并回答问题。

Activity 2：Reading

厘清人物关系，梳理故事情节。

1. 学生自主阅读文本，寻找故事的基本要素：main characters、time、main plot。

2. 小组合作，借助“故事山”确定文本的 introduction、rising action、climax、falling action、ending 以及情感线。

3. 结合教材中的练习，识记、运用文章中用于描写动作的词汇和短语。

本活动结合课本的练习、图片和动物动作，运用多模态的方式，帮助学生识记单词。首先小组合作，讨论自主阅读时找到的故事基本要素，提取和总结信息，这样有利于提升学生的思维品质和合作学习能力。学生运用“故事山”的方式梳理文本的基本情节，厘清故事的开端、发展和高潮。这一活动帮助学生学会提取有用信息，整合并内化语言知识，同时也为续写故事做铺垫。

Activity 3：Presentation

展示与分享学习成果，分析成果，判断合理性。

学生展示小组活动“故事山”成果。同学和老师评价故事发展和高潮的界定是否合适，并推敲故事的情感线。

Activity 4：Writing

迁移创新，合理续写故事。

在题目设置上，读后续写分为两段，分别给出故事情节。文本的最后一句话，作为续写第一段的开头句。第二段的开头句设置为婴儿哭泣，让学生续写 Prince Llewllyn 得知孩子依然存活后的言行和思考。续写故事应体现标题 *The Faithful Dog* 中的 Faithful 一词，并与原文的主题和语言风格一致。同时，学生应注重文章中动作的描写。

这一环节中，学生需要积极思考，调动已有的语言知识，续写出合理的故事。这也是创造性写作，锻炼学生的创新思维能力。学生可以借助 FASTHS（见 P132）扩充故事情节。

Para. 1: Then, with a final whimper, Gelert lay down and died.

Para. 2: All of a sudden, the loud baby crying drew the Prince's attention.

	Think (1)	Act	Say	Think (2)	Hear
Para. 1					
Para. 2					

Activity 5: Evaluation

评价续写故事，润色习作语言。

续写故事后，同学之间交换作文并互评，借鉴同学作文在内容上和语言上的优势，并根据评价量表指出不足。

评价量表包含内容合理性、语言和卷面三个维度，学生需要给出明确的可操作的修改意见。

Criteria	Yes	No	Further Improvement
Is the handwriting neat and tidy?			
Is the plot readable and reasonable?			
Is there any spelling or grammatical mistakes?			
Are there various complex language structures?			
Are there advanced words about actions and thoughts as well as proper linking words?			

（四）技巧归纳

读后续写部分，要求学生根据第一、二段的第一句话续写出完整且合理的故事，解决原文中的冲突和矛盾，给出合适的结尾。文章字数要求 150 词左右，即两个段落分别为 75 词左右。

读后续写可分为五步完成，即“读文章—读首句—构情节—扩细节—润语言”。关于“读文章”我们已经在“精研文本”部分做了说明，下面我们从第二步开始做说明。

☆第二、三步：读首句，构情节

“读首句，构情节”指根据文章和续写第一、二段首句中给出的已知信息（given information），构思第一、二段分别要阐明的新信息和新的故事情节（new information），即 Given-New Strategy，也称为 GN 策略。步骤如下：

1）确定第二段的结局即全文的结局；

2）由第一、二段首句确定第一段结尾的情节；

3）由第一段首句和构思的第一段的结尾确定第一段的情节；

4）由第二段首句和确定好的结局情节构思第二段的中间内容。

GN 策略构思方法和“汉堡包”构思方法相似，即确定开始和结局，再扩充细节信息。

以 2022 年嘉兴模拟题为例：

1）由文本信息可知，文章讲的是 Farhan 骑自行车失控时，姐姐不计前嫌、救助弟弟的故事。

2）由第一段第一句（Suddenly, Farhan lost control of the bicycle, heading in the direction of the girls, toward the stream.）可以推测出，弟弟有可能撞到其他女孩。但是，由第二段第一句（Farhan looked at Aminah, then at his bicycle, then back at his sister.）可知，Farhan 对姐姐的情绪发生了变化。因此，第一段主要描写姐姐如何奋不顾身救弟弟。

3）第一段主要描述具体的救助过程、心理活动以及其他小伙伴的反应和做法。

4）第二段主要情节涉及弟弟的心理变化和对姐姐的感激之情。

☆**第四步:扩细节**

在进行读后续写教学时,笔者发现经过一段时间的训练,学生基本能做到情节合理,但是在语言表达上和细节描写上还相当欠缺。因此,“扩细节”是教师教学和学生写作尤其要关注的部分。接下来讲述扩细节常见的几种方式。

A. To show, not to tell

在进行细节描写时,注重展示不同动作,而不是直接告知信息。该技巧要求学生有扎实的词汇基础,因此学生在学习时应多注意细节描写的传递和词汇的积累。

例1:

To tell: I took my bag, closed the door and went to school this morning.

To show: I grabbed my bag, slammed the door and dashed to school this morning.

例2:

To tell: The man walked out of the room.

To show:

The old man staggered out of the room.

Some innocent kids danced out of the room.

The young girl sailed out of the room.

A thief slipped out of the room.

新概念英语教材中一些关于细节描写的例子:

Suddenly, I saw the officer's **face light up**. He had spotted a tiny bottle at the bottom of my case and he **pounced on it with delight**.

"Perfume, eh?" he **asked sarcastically**. "You should have declared that. Perfume is not exempt from import duty."

"But it isn't perfume," I said. "It's hair gel." Then I **added with a smile**, "It's a strange mixture I make myself."

As I expected, he did not believe me. "Try it!" I said **encouragingly**.

该部分用 face light up、with delight 和 ask sarcastically 描述了海关工作人员发现我携带“违禁物品”时的喜悦和傲慢,描写细腻,生动形象。由于确定没有携带违禁物品,我很自信,文中用短语 add with a smile 和副词 encouragingly 来刻画这种情绪。

The man **let out a cry** and **jumped back several paces**. When Mrs Richards walked towards him, he **fled**, **slamming the door** behind him.

例句中使用 cry、jump back 展现角色受到惊吓时的本能反应。flee 和 slam the door 则刻画了角色害怕时仓皇逃走的样子。

进行动作描写时,应采用具体形象、生动的词汇,这就要求学生在学习中注意积累人、动物的相关动作表达。

比如喂宠物食物时,猫与人接近的动作:

The cat **walked straight over** to me, **nuzzling** and **licking my hand** in gratitude.

再比如看电视时,宠物依偎在身旁的温馨画面:

Whenever I watched television, the cat would **sit at my feet** and **purr loudly**.

再如心理描写,可借助肢体语言来进行扩充:

To tell: I was excited/delighted.

To show: My eyes twinkled/shone/glittered/sparkled with pleasure.

My heart was brimming over with joy.

I cheered, clapping my hands and jumping to my feet with excitement.

更多细节展示如下图:

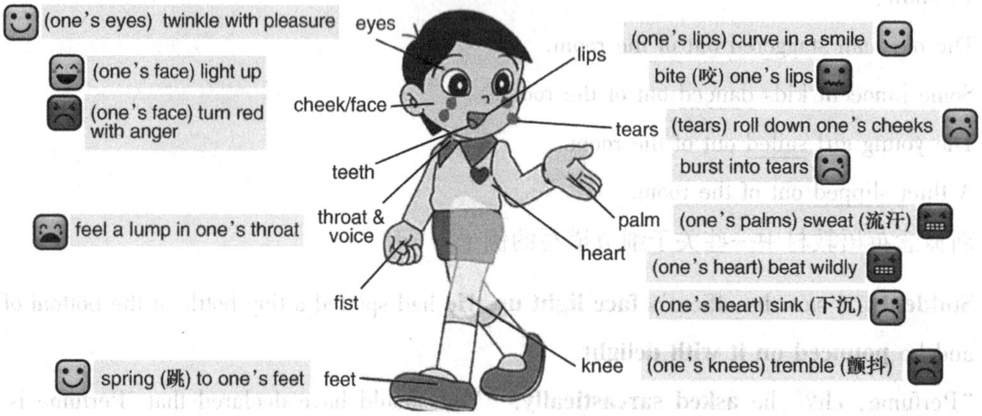

关于头部动作的描写

1) All sorts of **threads of my thoughts were messing up** my brain **when** the thought card came back to me.

2) **What kept lingering in my mind** was the deep regret about writing those words and the **intense** anxiety to get Dr. Simon's response.

3) **Fidgeting in my seat**, **I lowered my head**, not daring to look at him straight in the eyes.

4) **A mixed feeling of excitement and astonishment crept on** Bob's **mind**.

5) **Head drooping low**, I prepared myself for being condemned and scolded.

6) At this time, Missy, who had been **lowering her head in true regret and shame**, walked up and apologized for her mistake, **followed by** my explanation of our good intention.

7）The Lord High Chamerlain **wiped his forehead** with a handkerchief and then blew his **nose loudly**…"Let me see, now." He **glanced** at the list, **frowning**.

关于喉咙的描写

1）Anxiety hovering in my mind, I **felt the tightness in my throat with the eagerness for** Dr. Simon's response.

2）**Feeling/With a lump in my throat**, I cautiously unwrapped the envelope **with my fingers vibrating violently**.

关于声音的描写

1）**Voice of doubt and hesitation** echoed inside my mind like thunder. "What if I had failed?" I **whispered** to myself.

2）Eyes narrowed and fists clenched, I read the letter **in a trembling voice**.

关于手部动作的描写

1）Almost after what seemed like an eternity, I picked the card up, **not daring to flip it over**, with my **hand trembling**, heart pounding and mind racing, worrying about the upcoming reckoning.

2）My mind raced feverishly, with my **palms sweating** and my heart beating strongly.

3）**My hand seizing** the card tightly, I inched into his office, my heart beating fiercely.

4）With **my hands trembling** involuntarily, I finished the rest of the letter, only to find that I was invited to make a presentation on the award ceremony.

5）Annemaire **wiped her eyes with the back of her hand**.

6）The man from the West **unfolded** the little piece of paper handed to him. His hand was steady when he began to read, but it **trembled a little** by the time he had finished.

7）He **reached out his arms** and hugged me tightly, promising he would change the way he treated me from then on.

关于心理活动的描写

1）The instant I stepped onto the stage, all my endeavors as well as Mrs. Zhang's inspiration turned into the **solid confidence lying in my heart**.

2）I gave her a broad hug tightly **with a ripple of excitement exploding in my heart**.

3）**Heart pounding**, I carefully opened it to find a beautifully embossed certificate announcing that I had achieved first place in the regional mathematics competition.

4）While Missy rejoiced silently, I **was pierced to the heart** by overwhelming guilt and an inner voice urged me to **stick to my morality**.

关于眼部动作的描写

1）Every time I **looked into his eyes**, I felt like sitting on pins and needles.

2）I held my breath, **opened** my eyes wide and attentively **read** the card word by word.

3）A glimmer of appreciation **lit up** Robert's **eyes**.

4）Bob looked at Robert, **with eyes full of confusion mingled with exhilaration**.

5）Earnestly **looking at us in the eye**, the fatherly man hardened his voice and laid out what would never be erased from my mind.

6）The Lord High Chamberlain was a large, fat man who wore thick glasses which **made his eyes seem twice as big** as they really were…"The moon?" exclaimed the Lord High Chamberlain, **his eyes widening**.

关于面部表情的描写

1）With **a wave of happiness surging through** my body, I rushed to Dr. Simon's office, extending my sincere gratitude for what he suggested with a wide smile on my face.

2）With tears **rolling down** my face, bittersweet memories flooded into my mind—the cheering shouts on my birthday party, the smiling face he gave to me every single day and my rough words…

3）Looking at the money, Bob felt a sense of warmth welling up inside his body **with tears of gratitude streaming down his cheeks**.

4）When Bob looked at the sign "Smiling Pizza", he can't help but **beam a warm smile** at Robert. It is this smile that once melted Robert's heart and it will spill over to lighten up more faces.

5）When Bob gave the money to the server, all of them **cheered up with a truly warm smile**.

6）She **smiled a little**, though her **face** was **drawn with pain** and she **bit** her **lip**, the **smile fading**.

7）The man in the door way struck a match and lit his cigar. The light showed **a pale, square-jawed face with keen eyes**, and **a little scar near his right eyebrow**.

B. FASTHS 塑造人物形象

读后续写故事多为写人叙事的记叙文，为了更加完整地扩充细节，刻画人物性格，可以围绕主人公所感（Feel）、所做（Act）、所说（Say）、所思（Think）、所闻（Hear）、所见（See）（FASTHS）进行。

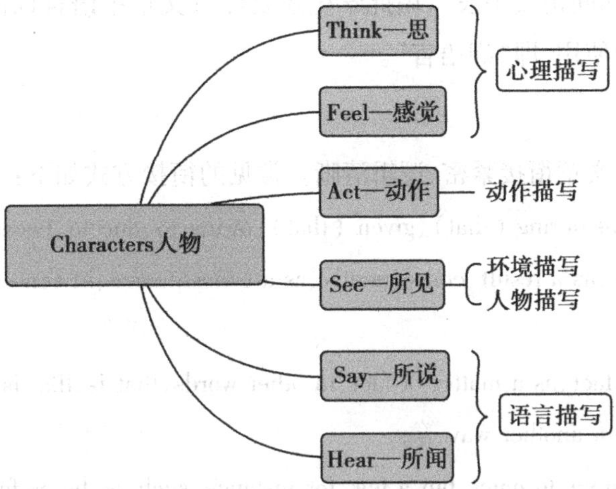

以 2023 年 1 月浙江卷读后续写中续写的第一段为例：

A few weeks later, I went to the farm again. The moment my car approaching it, **my thoughts** drifted back. Memories about freeing the hummingbird from the spider's web came flooding back. I **rushed back** to the once abandoned house. It was such a **comfort** that the **original hole** in the window was nowhere to be found. **Leaving** the house, I **couldn't help wondering** what its life was like now. Had **it** managed to **find its way back home**, or was it still living somewhere else **struggling to survive**?

作者几周后进入农场，围绕 FASTHS 展开描述。“我”进入农场后，思绪（Think）飘回了营救蜂鸟的过程，并情不自禁地为它担忧，体现了“我”对蜂鸟的关爱和担心。看见（See）曾经困住蜂鸟的“洞”已经修好，心里感受到了安慰（Feel）。“我”快速回到（Act）那个废弃的房子，细腻的动作描写衬托了我的担心和忧虑。

Think	My thoughts drifted back I couldn't help wondering…
Feel	a comfort
See	The original hole was nowhere to be found
Act	I: rushed back, leave the house, free the hummingbird
	The bird: find its way back home, struggle to survive

☆第五步：润语言

读后续写的评分标准提及“使用了多样且恰当的词汇和语法结构，表达流畅”“自然有效地使用了段落间、句间衔接手段”，因此学生还要注意文章中语言词汇和句型句式的丰富性和有效衔接方式的使用，即“润语言”。

A. 衔接手段

衔接词的使用使文章衔接紧密、逻辑清晰。常见的衔接方式如下：

1）因果关系：considering（that）、given（that）、owing to、due to、because of、on account of、as a result of、therefore、as a result、consequently、as a consequence、in consequence、thereby、thus、so 等；

2）解释说明：in fact、as a matter of fact、in other words、that is、that is to say、namely、to put it differently、to put it in another way 等；

3）举例：for example、to name but a few、for instance、such as、be as follows 等；

4）时间顺序：first、second、third、（soon）afterwards、meanwhile、finally、at first、in the beginning、subsequently、at last、in the end、eventually 等；

5）空间顺序：on one side… on the other side、on the opposite side、in front of、in the center of、in the distance、in the middle of、at the back of、on/to the left/right、close to、next to、nearby、beyond 等；

6）段落起始：generally speaking、to begin/start with、first and foremost、initially、first of all、in the first place、as we know、as is known to all 等；

7）递进或补充：in addition、additionally、furthermore、also、moreover、what's more、besides、to make matters worse、worse still、more/most importantly、last but not least、above all 等；

8）段落总结：to sum up、in conclusion、in a word、in summary、all in all、overall 等；

9）强调：certainly、indeed、above all、surely、to tell（you）the truth、exactly 等；

10）转折：but、yet、however、nonetheless、nevertheless 等；

11）对比：similarly、in contrast、contrary to、whereas、whilst、while、instead、instead of、like、unlike、in the same way 等；

12）表达观点：personally（speaking）、from my perspective、in my opinion、I'm fully convinced that、as far as I am concerned、in my view、from my point of view、take the stand that 等。

B. 使用习语或俗语

1）No matter what happens to her，Mrs. Lin always seems to be **a happy camper**.（乐天派）

2）I **hit the ceiling/floor** when I found him lie.（勃然大怒）

3）He **got hot under the collar** when he was asked to be responsible for what he had done.（勃然大怒）

4) If I'm late again, my head teacher will **go bananas**. (抓狂)

5) Constant dropping wears the stone. 滴水穿石。

6) It is never too old to learn. 活到老学到老。

7) My neighbor's loud music after midnight is really **like a red rag to a bull**. (使人极其愤怒)

C. 使用非谓语

1) Sensing the rage creeping to my spine, I was particularly worried that my son would be barked and bitten by the dog, and memories of being attacked by animals came flooding back.

2) He rushed directly to the squirrel, trying his absolute best to free it from the thorns.

3) Frozen to the spot, Daniel racked his brains, attempting to figure out a solution to tackle this unexpected situation.

4) Hearing the squirrel's faint voice filled with pain, Daniel was heartbroken.

5) Looking at his watch, he saw that it was one o'clock.

6) Armed with a torch, the vicar went up into the clock tower to see what was going on.

7) Not wanting to frighten the poor man, Mrs Richards quickly hid in the small store-room under the stairs.

8) She tried to explain the situation, saying "It's only me," but it was too late.

9) When Mrs Richards walked towards him, he fled, slamming the door behind him.

10) Ashamed of having acted so rashly, Dimitri apologized to Aleko for having accused him.

11) Despite its immensity, it is both simple and elegant, fulfilling its designer's dream to create "an enormous object drawn as faintly as possible".

12) We welcome the seasons by the riverside, crowning the youngest girl with flowers in the spring, holding a summer festival on Midsummer Eve, giving thanks for the harvest in the autumn, and throwing a holly into the current in the winter.

13) I draw back to the town and began to retrace the route, taking frequent glances at the map.

14) The girl asked to see a timetable, feeling sure that her father could not have made such a mistake.

D. 使用独立主格

1) The girl, tears streaming down her face, begged to be allowed to slip into the guard's van.

2) Then her composure regained, she was ready to set off with the porter's assistance to

search for any intruders who might still be lurking in her flat.

3) Hands sweating, I moved away from the coach to protect my son, only to find that a scorpion was making its way to Evan.

4) Heart pounding and mind racing, he failed to utter a single word only to be touched by the honest and sincere emotional connection between the human and animals which is called love.

5) He was adjusting his camera lens when a squirrel jumped into his sight, its eyes glistening like a gem and uttering a cry of excitement.

6) Heart beating fiercely, memories of helping the squirrel came flooding back.

7) Tears blurring his sights, Daniel would remember the scene forever, which showed the deep love and trust between a kind soul and the animals.

E. with 复合结构

1) According to my father, I should be looking at the farms and cottages in a valley, with the spire of the church of our village showing in the far distance.

2) With my heart pounding violently, I could hardly suppress my worst thought that my son might be attacked.

3) With a still thumping heart, I exhaled a sigh of relief.

4) The little squirrel, with its paw bleeding heavily, calmed down, as if knowing Daniel would save it.

5) Putting away his camera at once, Daniel tried to seek assistance in all directions, with a hint of worry flickering in his eyes.

6) At the sight of Daniel, the squirrel leaped onto his palm with its eyes glistening with a glow of excitement and gratitude.

F. 使用动作链

1) Suddenly, Bailey, who had been scanning the scorpion cautiously, went up, pushed it to the ground with his strong paws and cracked it into half with his sharp teeth within a second.

2) Overwhelmed by immense gratitude and relief, I patted, kissed Bailey's head and embraced him tightly.

3) Without hesitation, Daniel released the trapped squirrel, gently carried it in his cupped hands and dashed to his car to give it first aid treatment.

4) Suppressing the grief in his heart, Daniel gently stroked the quivering squirrel, pulled the thorns out of its bleeding paw and cleaned its wound with some new leaves.

5) Walking swiftly towards it, Daniel cleaned its paw with a cloth, applied some medicine to the wound and then covered the wound with great care.

6) On his way to the sweet shop, he dropped his six pence and it rolled along the pavement and then disappeared down a drain. George took off his jacket, rolled up his sleeves and pushed his right arm through the drain cover. He could not find his sixpence anywhere, and what is more, he could not get his arm out.

7) We resolve to get up earlier each morning, eat less, find more time to play with the children, and do a thousand and one jobs about the dog for a walk every day.

8) Her first impulse was to go round all the rooms looking for the thieves, but then she decided that at the age it might be more prudent to have someone with her, so she went to fetch the porter from the basement.

9) Suddenly, my father appeared to be worried; he retreated a few steps, stared at his family gathered around the old shell opener, and quickly came toward us. He seemed very pale, with a peculiar look. In a low voice, he said to my mother.

G. 使用无灵主语

1) A sense of guilt and shame overwhelmed me.

2) A wave of terror tore me into pieces.

3) A rush of ecstasy and emotion swept his spine.

4) A ripple of anxiety flooded through my body, when I was about to receive my card, wondering what would be written on it.

5) A wave of happiness surged through my body and I couldn't wait to tell Dr. Simon the good news and express my sincere gratitude to him.

6) A pang of guilt and regret washing over me, I painfully struggled with the internal conflict of loyalty to my friend and the moral dilemma of maintaining a lie.

7) An enormous sense of guilt arose in me as his stern eyes seemed to proclaim me as the "guilty" bystander.

8) Words poured out the moment I met my father, from the misery of being corrected all the time, to my struggling to win his support.

9) The next few minutes witnessed how Missy muttered the whole truth.

10) As we approached the breakwater, a violent desire seized me once more to see my Uncle Jules, to be near him, to say to him something consoling, something tender.

11) The noise from Blossom, forgotten, unmilked, comfortable, in the barn, had sent

Annemarie warily out with the milking bucket.

12) An all-night party on New Year's Eve provided me with a good excuse for not carrying out either of these new resolutions on the first day of the new year.

H. 使用形容词和副词

1) Surprised and touched, Bob failed to utter a single word, his jaw nearly dropping to the ground. Never had he thought that his seemingly random acts could mean so much.

2) Amazed but worried, Bob refused the money firmly, saying: "I just assume my responsibility and do what I want to."

3) Slowly and carefully, I opened the envelope and began to read.

4) Slowly and nervously, Missy began to expand on the story she had made up, her voice quivering with fear.

5) My father seemed absolutely bewildered. He murmured: What a catastrophe! Suddenly growing furious, my mother exclaimed: ...Astonished, my sisters were awaiting their father.

6) Aware of these pitfalls, this year I attempted to keep my resolutions to myself.

I. 倒装句式

1) At the corner stood a drug store, brilliant with electric lights.

2) Once upon a time, in a kingdom by the sea, there lived a little princess named Lenore.

3) Next came a horse, swimming bravely, but we were afraid that the strength of the current would prevent its landing anywhere before it became exhausted.

4) Only in a separsely-populated rural community is it possible to disregard it.

5) Hardly had I pictured the terrifying scenes of Evan being hurt by Bailey when I spotted a scorpion on the carpet, 5 inches away from where Evan was crawling.

6) So ashamed was I that blood rushed to my face, leaving me tongue-tied and red-faced.

7) Hadn't it been for Bailey's bravery, I would possibly have suffered the sorrowful loss of my baby.

8) Hardly had he stepped into the forest when he caught sight of that squirrel scampering around them.

9) Beyond his wildest dreams was the sight that the squirrel was waiting for him with many flowers and nuts.

10) Scared as I was, I managed to summon up some courage and overturned the card with trembling fingers.

11) So ashamed was I that I could feel the blood rush to my face.

12) Never had I pictured the man who trusted me more than his own daughter casting such a piercing look at me.

J. 虚拟语气

1) But for/Without her selfless instruction, I couldn' t have got the first prize of the competition.

2) Had she not insisted that I take up the challenge, I wouldn' t have progressed so significantly.

3) If you were to ask Harry what was in the bottle, he would tell you that it contained perfume mud. If you expressed doubt or surprise, he would immediately invite you to smell it and then to rub some into your skin. This brief experiment would dispel any further doubts you might have.

K. 强调句式

1) It was not until I caught sight of the scorpion that I realized that the dog was trying his best to save my son instead of attacking him.

2) It was Bailey that taught me if you treat animals with heartfelt kindness, they will become your trustworthy friends.

3) It was the bad experience that enabled me to realize that love and kindness, a lack of which would lead to prejudice, finally bridged the gap between Bailey and me as well as enhanced our relationship.

4) It was when Daniel was about to leave that the squirrel swayed its fluffy tails in front of Daniel, indicating him to notice the ground.

5) After jumping about on the carpet and twisting the human frame into uncomfortable positions, I sat down at the breakfast table in an exhausted condition. It was this that betrayed me.

L. 使用修辞方法

明喻

1) His comforting words were like sunlight penetrating through darkness, leaving Daniel exhaling a sigh of relief.

2) Rage flowed through like lava.

3) His hair is as dark as the hyacinth-blossom, and his lips are red as the rose of his desire; but passion has made his face like pale ivory, and sorrow has set her seal upon his brow.

4) "Tell me as soon as you have finished," said Johnsy, closing her eyes and lying white and still as a fallen statue.

5) Suddenly a raft appeared, looking rather like Noah's ark, carrying the whole family, a few hens, the dogs, a cat and a bird in the cage.

借喻

1) Love is a wonderful thing. It is more precious than emeralds, and dearer than fine opals.

2) My roses are white, as white as the foam of the sea, and whiter than the snow upon the mountain.

3) My roses are yellow, as yellow as the hair of the mermaiden who sits upon an amber throne, and yellower than the daffodil that blooms in the meadow before the mower comes with his scythe.

4) My roses are red, as red as the feet of the dove, and redder than the great fans of coral that wave and wave in the ocean-cavern.

暗喻

1) Every time I looked into her father's eyes I felt like sitting on pins and needles.

2) The city is a jungle.

3) The mind is a ocean.

4) He was the apple of her eye.

5) They had a skeleton in the cupboard.

6) The dog is stone dead.

7) Silas is a coach potato.

夸张

1) After what seemed like eternity, Bailey rushed to the scorpion and crushed it to death by its paws, with brave and determined barking.

2) After what seemed like a century, he said slowly but firmly: "It's really kind of you. But it's too much."

3) I was about to explode.

4) She had lived in the flat for thirty years and was a veritable magpie at hoarding, and it seemed as though everything she possessed had been tossed out and turned over and over.

拟人

1) Bailey seemed to sense my friendliness to him, shaking his tail happily and staring at me with kindness.

2) He sat there quietly, keeping his head up and swayed his tail, as if to expect Lisa's praise.

重复

1) Night after night have I sung of him, though I knew him not; Night after night have I told his stories to the stars.

2) If I bring her a red rose, she will dance with me till dawn. If I bring her a red rose, I shall hold her in my arms, and she will lean her head upon my shoulder...

3) But the tree shook its head... But the tree shook its head... But the tree shook its head.

4) It was my dad who walked me through adversity, it was he who grabbed my shoulders that I achieved my ambitions, and it was he who sacrificed his time and money and more importantly, his love to bring me up.

5) His wife liked him. She liked the deadly serious way he received any complaints. She liked the way he wanted to serve her. She liked the way he felt about being a hotel-keeper. She liked his old, heavy face and big hands.

M. 使用环境描写

1) Sunshine slanted though the window, melting the ice between us and moistening our hearts.

2) As the moon slowly rose, the conversation smoothly went on, all the misunderstandings vanishing without trace.

3) The night was quiet, too. A slight breeze moved in the tops of the trees, and from across the meadow came the sound of the sea's movement, which was a constant sound here and had always been... There were stars here and there, dotting the sky among thin clouds, but no moon. Annemaire shivered, standing at the foot of the steps.

4) The time was barely 10 o'clock at night, but chilly gusts of wind with a taste of rain in them had well nigh depeopled the streets.

(五)迁移创新

作为高考新题型,读后续写给教师和学生都带来了巨大的挑战。2024 年高考,河南省高三学生第一次考核该题型,学生需要在平时强化练习,教师也应该对学生习作加以指导。以我校高三调研三为例,展示部分学生学习成果。该文本改编自 2023 年 6 月新课标 I 卷读后续写,即在老师鼓励下参加写作比赛,由 ChatGPT 生成。

During my high school years, my math teacher, Mrs. Zhang, noticed a spark in me whenever I tackled complex mathematical problems. She had been observing my progress throughout the year and was particularly impressed with my talent in abstract reasoning. One day, after class, she approached me with an intriguing proposal: to represent the school in a regional mathematics competition. Instantly, I hesitated and my mind raced back to a traumatic event from my primary school years—a quizbee where I had frozen on stage, forgetting everything I had prepared. The memory had stayed with me and left me with a fear of competitive scenarios. Mrs. Zhang seemed to sense my reservations and said, "Life is about facing our fears. Every challenge you encounter is an opportunity to grow. I truly believe you have what it takes to shine." With her words echoing in my ears and her unwavering belief as a driving force, I decided to face my past demons and take on the competition.

The theme for this year was geometry, a branch of mathematics that explores the dimensions of shapes and their features. My chosen topic was a complex theorem, known for its complicated patterns and strong logic. Although a challenging task, the theorem resonated with me deeply. I saw it as a metaphor for life—seemingly complex situations that, with the right perspective, could be simplified and understood. The following weeks were a blur of numbers, shapes, and formulas. I immersed myself in libraries, wrote notes everywhere, and had endless discussions with Mrs. Zhang. My first draft, when presented to her, was met with constructive feedback. "This is a recommendable effort," she said, "but I believe you can do better. Refine it." And so, again and again, my presentation evolved. Through this rigorous process, my once paralyzing fear of competition slowly transformed into a burning passion for understanding and exploration.

注意：

1. 续写词数应为150词左右；

2. 请按如下格式在答题卡的相应位置作答。

Para. 1: *Several weeks after my final submission, an official-looking envelope arrived at my home.*

Para. 2: *The day after the award ceremony, I found myself at the door of Mrs. Zhang's classroom.*

（六）作品舞台

学生作品 1

Several weeks after my final submission, an official-looking envelop arrived at my home. A shiver went down my spine and my feet, as if rooted to the ground, I could not move a bit. Heart thumping feverishly with anticipation, I opened the envelope with trembling hands. A letter fell out of it, which read "Congratulations...". Clenching the thin piece of paper, I stared at it with utter disbelief. The words "You have come first in this competition." didn't seem to make sense, yet a happy bubble began to rise inside my chest. Gradually, it dawned on me that I had, magically, overcame my fear and triumphed. The following days flew past like a dream with a ceremony and awards.

The day after the award ceremony, I found myself at the door of Mrs. Zhang's classroom. Taking a deep breath, I knocked on the door. All of a sudden, it was flung open and out running came Mrs. Zhang. Extending her arms to me, she shouted with pure happiness, "Yes! I know you'd make it!" I could barely conceal the smile on my face as she held me tight and stared deep into my eyes, with the sparkling light of pride in her eyes. "It was all because of you, Mrs. Zhang. Never would I ever have achieved this had you not spotted the spark in me or not been there, supporting my every humble step to overcome my fear." I choked out, tears brimming in my eyes. Mrs. Zhang wore a warm smile and whispered, stroking my hair, "I know you get what it takes."

教师点评：

这篇作文续写内容情节合理，与原文的协同性较高，很好地完成了写作任务。作文第一段描写了作者收到获奖通知时的紧张和难以置信，以及作者最终克服了内心对数学比赛的恐惧。第二段描写了作者参加颁奖典礼后，拜访老师，表达对老师的感激之情。

语言上，此篇习作运用了丰富的语法结构和较高级的词汇。语法上，出现了独立主格（第一段 Heart thumping feverishly with anticipation 与第二段 tears brimming in my eyes）、非谓语（第二段 taking a deep breath）、定语从句（第一段 which read）、主语从句（第一段 it dawned on me that...）和倒装（第二段 never would I ever have achieved this），展示了学生扎实的语法基础。此外，运用了夸张（as if rooted to the round）和比喻（flew past like a dream）的修辞手法，表达形象生动。词汇上，feverishly、with utter disbelief、gradually、magically 等副词和介词短语的使用，描写细腻，从不同程度上表达了"我"得奖时的难以置信。但是，"Never would I ever have achieved this had you not spotted the spark in me or not been there..."中两个倒装连续使用容易产生歧义，建议改为"I would never have achieved this had you not spotted the spark in me or not been there."。

学生作品 2

Several weeks after my final submission, an official-looking envelope arrived at my home. Too nervous to open the envelope, I stood still, my mind totally blank and my palms sweating. Taking a deep breath, I opened the envelope slowly with my trembling hands. I claimed the gold medal! My face split into a wide smile. I leaped about the room, overjoyed and shocked. The letter said that my presentation, whose abstract reasoning together with strong logic left the professors an impression, was excellent and informed me to attend the award ceremony. So delighted was I that I felt as if I had been in a dream. There was no doubt that it was Mrs. Zhang who helped me most.

The day after the award ceremony, I found myself at the door of Mrs. Zhang's classroom. A little embarrassed, I gave her a nervous smile. Mrs. Zhang's dimond eyes locked onto me and led me in happily. When informed of the news that I claimed the gold medal, Mrs. Zhang let out an utter of joy. I deeply appreciated her encouragement which gave me strength to overcome my demon as well as her constructive suggestions concerning my presentation. With her lips held in a steady smile, Mrs. Zhang said that it was my capability in maths together with my steady efforts that mattered. From the competition. I came to learn that under the guidence of people, you could always overcome your demons with effort.

学生互评：

这篇习作续写合理，心理描写和动作描写丰富，nervous、my mind blank、my palms sweating、trembling hands、overjoyed and shocked 等词汇传神地表达了“我”又惊又喜的状态。句式上，文章使用了强调句、倒装句等，句式丰富，突出了“我”对 Mrs. Zhang 的感激之情。美中不足的是文章有简单单词的拼写错误，如 guidence 应为 guidance，dimond 应为 diamond。这也是我们在写作中容易犯的错误。

参考文献

[1] 崔文华，唐书哲. 拉波夫叙事模式在高中英语读后续写中的建构和应用[J].中小学外语教学(中学篇)，2023，46(5)：7-12.

[2] 李芷莹，金檀. 英语阅读素材的数据驱动型改编：以 2022 年高考英语阅读素材为例[J]. 英语学习，2022(8)：36-42.

[3] 倪娜. 基于建构主义“支架”理论的初中英语写作教学研究[D]. 上海：上海师范大学，2012.

[4] 王初明. 语言习得过程:创造性构建抑或创造性模仿？[J].现代外语. 2021，44(5)：585-591.

[5] 文秋芳. “产出导向法”的中国特色[J]. 现代外语，2017，40(3)：348-358，438.

[6] 文秋芳. “产出导向法”与对外汉语教学[J]. 世界汉语教学，2018，32(3)：387-400.

[7] 杨峰. KWLSW 策略在高中英语写作教学中的应用研究[D]. 黄石：湖北师范大学，2023.

[8] 中华人民共和国教育部. 普通高中英语课程标准：2017 年版 2020 年修订[M]. 2 版. 北京：人民教育出版社，2020.